FINDING GRACE IN THE CONCERT HALL

FINDING GRACE IN THE CONCERT HALL

COMMUNITY & MEANING AMONG SPRINGSTEEN FANS

LINDA K. RANDALL

WAVELAND
PRESS, INC.
Long Grove, Illinois

For information about this book, contact:
Waveland Press, Inc.
4180 IL Route 83, Suite 101
Long Grove, IL 60047-9580
(847) 634-0081
info@waveland.com
www.waveland.com

For my sister, Edna, my hero,
who was always there for me,
and for my favorite monkey—
he knows who he is.

Contents

Foreword

Rediscovering Music and Meaning

Jeanne Simonelli
Wake Forest University

**And we, on the receiving end of that beautiful gift,
are ourselves rejuvenated . . . if not redeemed.**
(Jon Stewart honoring Bruce Springsteen,
Kennedy Center, December 2009)

I came of age in the sixties in New York City as a card-carrying hippie, but I was never much of a concert goer. While many of my friends inched up the New York State Thruway to Woodstock and Watkins Glen, I watched on TV from the comfort of my Lower East Side living room, chuckling at their folly. And while I wore out the vinyl on *Magical Mystery Tour* and dripped candle wax on Dylan's *Blonde on Blonde*, I wasn't big on Bruce Springsteen. Somewhere in the early seventies, I bought a copy of Springsteen's second album, *The Wild, The Innocent, and the E Street Shuffle*, but it was because, like many disillusioned hippies, I was leaving New York and wanted to take something of its spirit with me. Yet, as Springsteen describes in his November 2009 Madison Square Garden concert introduction to the album, half of the collection was about New Jersey, and the rest was his "romantic ideas and fantasies of New York City."

For the sixties music listener, music was about individual meaning. Enhanced by various and sundry mind-altering experiences, listening to a particular album track was a personal and unique journey. You could get lost in lyrics and rhythms, and stuck between the multicolored grooves, but for those not on the concert trail, it was something between the listener and the artist. Dead Heads notwithstanding, the notion of creating meaning in a fan *community* was not really part of the program.

Now, over 40 years later, Linda Randall's *Finding Grace in the Concert Hall: Community and Meaning among Springsteen Fans* takes the reader on a different kind of musical journey, one less about lyrics than about love—about the quest of twenty-first century wanderers to find a more extensive significance in the musical experience. As Randall's friend and longtime anthropology professor, I was amused and perplexed as she shyly revealed her growing involvement with Bruce Springsteen's music as a middle-aged concert aficionado. As time went by, packages began to arrive in the mail containing cassette copies of Springsteen albums, but with the exception of the *E-Street* standbys, it was difficult get into the newer material.

In December 2002 Springsteen played in Charlotte, North Carolina, an easy drive from where I now lived and taught in Winston-Salem. With little or no understanding of what the concert experience was really about, I went online and got us the cheapest pair of tickets available, close to the ceiling of the Charlotte Coliseum in what is known as the "nose-bleed section." I was unfamiliar with the specialized vocabulary of Springsteen viewing: GA (general admission) tickets, the Pit (the area in front of the stage), tailgates. You went to hear music. Right?

Wrong. The Charlotte Coliseum rocked. Like a first-time attendee at someone else's church, I watched as Linda and 20,000 others stood, swayed, raised hands, and sang out the lyrics of almost four hours of music. Even though I didn't really "get it," it was clear that something was going on among that body of people, something that paralleled the coming together of a group of churchgoers in what anthropologist Victor Turner calls *communitas*. As we drove back toward Winston-Salem post-concert at 1:00 AM, Linda explained a little more about the type of people of whom she was now becoming part, and about the broader culture of the Springsteen fan community.

The classic anthropological meaning of culture involves shared values and norms of behavior, which have been learned, patterned, and transmitted from generation to generation. While one normally associates culture with geography or ethnicity, in a rapidly globalizing world cultural groups crosscut these physical boundaries and extend to include those who share markers of identity and similarity that are no longer so narrowly constrained. Linda's growing involvement in the global Springsteen cultural community revealed a series of values that had little to do with music per se, and everything to do with finding and giving meaning in an increasingly complex world. As the pages that follow reveal, the Springsteen culture first found expression in the concert venues of the nation and the world. But though numerous fans count concerts as others once counted coup many of those who belong to the Springsteen global village never experience a live performance. For these, the burgeoning medium of the Internet—Web sites and chat rooms, YouTube and e-mail—allow for the creation of virtual communitas.

As much as I enjoyed the Charlotte show and had more understanding than most friends and family of Linda's growing "efangelism"—her desire to share what she was experiencing with those around her—it was still not entirely clear to me what it was that fans who crisscrossed the nation (and the globe) got out of the concert experience. As an anthropologist, I stepped back and watched this culture with the same kind of objectivity that I would apply to any field site, looking at individual and group interactions, and at the community's structure, function, and organization. As a friend and traveling companion, I was more than happy to have Linda identify and connect with "Bruce people" in almost every locale we visited from Sydney to Belfast to Paris. We met people she knew only from the "boards" (fan forums), and they opened their lives and schedules to us, touring us around their cities and inviting us to their homes. As will be explained later, trust among fanfriends is an integral part of the greater community.

Getting to know, trust, and be trusted is an important part of the field experience for anthropologists, and I encouraged Linda to apply the theory and method she had learned in completing an anthropology major to her continuing Bruce experience. Later, when she took the opportunity to pursue a graduate degree in Religion and Culture at Wake Forest University, it seemed a logical focus for her thesis, one that was about American Pop Culture at the same time as it was about belief and the need for meaning in community. As she widened the lens with which she viewed Springsteen's music and performances and the many-faceted relationships she was developing in the field of the fan community, I joined her in attending concerts when they were convenient.

It was especially interesting to watch the ways in which the community operationalized the Springsteen adage "nobody wins unless everybody wins." As a cultural anthropologist working with Zapatista communities in southern Mexico, I observed that their guiding precept was similar: "for each of us nothing; for all of us everything" (Earle and Simonelli 2005). As two dissimilar cultural groups struggling to make sense out of the complex millennial years, they were remarkably similar in the ways in which survival was structured: community, generosity, and an awful lot of music!

Linda completed her graduate studies in 2008, and I decided to preview her manuscript among the students in my "Peoples and Cultures of the World" class during fall 2009. In the class we read and discussed four other ethnographies about communities in Mexico, Africa, Palestine, and Native America. We explored the enormous economic, social, and health obstacles faced by those described in the books. Why then, were we reading about the search for meaning in affluent America and beyond? First, because middle-class America *is* a people and culture of the world. Second, because Wake Forest University students were often raised in conservative and religious families. While many of these students were still participants in the organized religions of their childhood, others were experiencing a search for less-structured meaning, as should be a part of attending college. For both groups, the text resonated. We watched and listened to Bruce clips designed to illustrate the main points of the book: finding community, helping others, developing trust, and listening to the individual and group message of the music. As one student noted:

> Although being introduced to Bruce Springsteen at a young age, I had never thought of him to be a religious-type figure. However, after reading this essay I see that many musicians have the ability to draw a following through their words and shows. . . . Also, I found the current religion discussion to be very intriguing. To think that those who are becoming disaffiliated with their family religion and clinging onto nature, or in this case Bruce, as alternatives was very fascinating. The philanthropy section solidified the argument for me. The fact that Bruce "preaches" at his shows to go out and help others, while also connecting to some inner feeling within his fans solidified his place on the pulpit. . . . I found it to be the most intriguing work we have read so far in the class.

In the midst of our reading, Springsteen played in Charlotte again. We called it a cultural event, had a lottery for five tickets, still up in the nose-bleed section, and packed into the Anthropology van to take a class trip into the ethnographic field. Once again, Charlotte rocked. Returning to class, we discussed the integration of religion, community, and social support. We transitioned from talking about dastardly life situations, in which people are struggling to achieve a decent material life, to one in which people whose material lives are secure (mostly) are struggling to put meaning into the material.

As this book will show, Bruce-fans are a community, a loose alliance of people united by common identity, who have come together to facilitate a transformation in some aspect of life—social, economic, political. Linda Randall describes how this works in the upcoming pages. She allows the reader to explore the personal and group implications of "belonging," as well as how religion works within contemporary society. In the text, her Bruce friends speak about conversion, redemption, epiphanies, faith, and the ways in which ritual and rites of intensification connect them together. She says:

Seekers find their own way across this landscape, searching for that transcendent moment, that feeling of connection and inclusion, that one "face that ain't looking through me" ("Badlands"). . . . "Converts" see their own experiences reflected in Springsteen's words. His honesty and the hope highlighted in his songs provide members of the "congregation" with the tools—philosophy, philanthropy, compassion—to cope in an increasingly inhospitable society. Devotees find solace in these songs in much the same way that devoutly practicing religious people find solace in the sacred texts of their religions. There is a Springsteen line appropriate for most any event.

And what about me? Have I been converted? Am I a fan? I must confess that when it was announced in November 2009 that Springsteen would play the entire sequence of songs from the 1972 album *The Wild, The Innocent, and the E Street Shuffle* at a Madison Square Garden concert, I went online to look for a cheap flight to New York. After all, E Street had been the music of my New York hippie home; the underlying rhythm of shared fantasies. Unable to come up with a flight, I had to be satisfied with listening to the song "4th of July, Asbury Park (Sandy)" almost live by cell phone.

At a recent set of extraordinary concerts at the Meadowlands in New Jersey, I did have my own set of epiphanies. First, I rediscovered music in general. No longer will I walk into my house, converse with the dogs, and turn on the TV for companionship. Like the character who remembers too late that "I Coulda Had a V-8," I've dug out all the old cassettes (yes, cassettes) and have begun to fill the space with rhythm and harmony, lyrics, and . . . meaning. And as there *is* a Springsteen line appropriate for most any event, that weekend's variety of songs about hometowns and long roads home, played out against the background of the New York metropolitan area accents that I left behind, have convinced me that it's time to go "home."

Randall confronts the dilemma of finding meaning in music in the initial pages of this book, noting: "He identified with my struggles and frustrations, while not waiting for me to identify with him, and perhaps that is his talent and genius. Bruce places the onus of understanding on himself, and not the listener. His job is to convince us that he knows what we know, to provide us with hope, and not to ask us to understand him." For the Springsteen community and its surrounding culture, this "reflects both [the fans'] emotional and spiritual attachment as well as their attempts to live according to the moral precepts they find through this music."

The ties that bind people together in culture and community are no longer only those described in traditional community ethnographies of village peoples in far-away jungles and deserts. *Finding Grace* is an ethnography of popular culture in a complex world that has become connected by travel, the Internet, and as seen here, the multiple messages of Bruce Springsteen's 30-plus-year body of music.

Acknowledgments

*W*hen I returned to school to earn my master's degree in fall 2006, it never entered my mind to explore my feelings about Bruce Springsteen. But with encouragement and guidance from my academic mentors, Dr. Jeanne Simonelli and Dr. Lynn Neal, this project began to take shape. Along the way, I managed to convert one of these two wonderful women to the Church of Bruce; a 50-percent conversion rate is excellent by any missionary standard!

My journey through the countryside of Springsteen nation brought me many new friends and experiences, and I thank all the fine citizens for their companionship and support. In particular, I thank the members of the various message boards—*greasylake.org, backstreets.com, stoneponylondon.net, thunderroad.com,* and *brucespringsteen.net. CmonMrTrouble,* you sent me my very first concert recording and are responsible for my addiction; *Haggerb,* thank you for not being a psycho killer and for providing me with a solid basis for trusting my Internet friends *in real life.* The list of those to whom I owe thanks is long.

Thanks goes out also to the members of Dr. Simonelli's anthropology class who read my thesis and submitted many good ideas for revision. Students wanted more first-person accounts and stories, and I have tried to supply those.

My concert-going partner in crime, *cruisin'tobruce,* also deserves my gratitude for sharing expenses and experiences with me all over the Eastern Seaboard as well as some mid-America excursions. She tolerated me well, right up until the last time I forgot the tickets.

I also must recognize the persistent assistance I received from my pal and companion Zero, my Maine coon cat, who spent hours hanging over my keyboard as I typed. I attribute all typos and errors to his help, and thank him for the opportunity to lay the blame at his paws.

And lastly, my thanks and gratitude go out to Mr. Bruce Frederick Springsteen, a man of heart and of conscience who constantly keeps me honest and aware that *"it ain't no sin to be glad you're alive"* ("Badlands").

To any readers who may be future converts to the Church of Bruce I say—I envy you. To be able to experience the awe and depth of feeling of a new convert is an amazing experience, and it only happens once. Enjoy, and welcome to Springsteen nation.

If you want to be free, there is but one way;
It is to guarantee an equally full measure of
liberty to all your neighbors. There is no other.

—Carl Shurz

Bruce Springsteen, Madison Square Garden, New York City
(Photo by Danny Clinch/Contour by Getty Images)

Introduction

The artist enriches the soul of humanity. The artist delights people with a thousand unsuspected shades of feeling. The artist reveals spiritual riches until then unknown, and gives people new reasons for loving life, new inner lights to guide them. (Rodin)

*T*his is not a book analyzing lyrics, a critical dissection of chords and tonalities, or a comparison of musical forms. This began as an exercise in introspection, a way for me to examine my reactions and emotional connection to one man's music and to explore the spiritual terrain of my own soul. In the process, I realized that the ways in which I processed the music were not unique to me, and I began to look around at other fans. What I found was a community, rich in variation and experience but sharing common values and characteristics.

I have always known that I was a by-product of rock and roll. My older sisters influenced me at a very young age with their musical choices. They were already teenagers when I was born, and my lullabies were popular songs sung by Elvis, Bill Haley, Chuck Berry, and Little Richard. I am of the generation that used rock 'n' roll, the music of *our* times, to mark our milestones, to commemorate benchmarks, and to punctuate events. Music seemed somehow more real back then—no digital mediums at all, just vinyl circles spinning round and round, and the sounds of those circles playing endlessly on our radios. If we played our music on our own record players, we experienced the music tactilely as well as audibly—this was music you could hold in your hand, running fingers over the grooves that spun the magic into sounds. It was young music, and we were young. Now, the music is no longer young, no longer comes via vehicles we can touch and feel and sometimes shatter. Now music is a string of ones and zeros, for the most part, served up digitally and without liner notes (remember them?). And we are now AARP members . . . but that music, that old time rock and roll, is still ours.

Dozens of books have been written about Bruce Frederick Joseph Springsteen, and while it is necessary to discuss the man himself in order to connect the dots, my focus is on Mr. Springsteen's fans, the things that they share, and the community they have created. I will not be comparing Springsteen fans with Beatle fans or U2 fans—that is not my intent; this is not a cross-cultural analysis, a comparison of cultures. Grateful Dead fans may well create worlds in the parking lots of arenas; Tom Petty fans may organize tailgate parties; and Phish phanatics may trek across multiple state lines to see the band play. I am not personally involved in any of those fan communities, but I am an active participant and citizen of Springsteen nation, a bona fide Tramp (as in "tramps like us, baby we were born to run"), a Springsteen fan who gathers to mingle with others of like mind to devour and savor the music. With one show under my belt prior to 1999, I have since seen Bruce Springsteen—with and without the E Street Band—somewhere in the vicinity of 70 times. I have traveled to nine states and two European countries for shows, and I have met fans in another five countries. I have been a true participant observer over these past ten years, in the perfect position to watch, listen, discuss, interview, and experience right alongside devoted fans of all ages, nationalities, and political leanings. My interest and background in anthropology provided me with the tools to observe and document, while my fascination with both religion and popular culture gave me the lens through which to see and the framework on which to hang my metaphorical hat. But the real heart of my research comes from the fans, their experiences, and their generosity in sharing their hearts with me, and with each other.

My approach to the subject matter differs from other authors of Springsteen material, not because of any stunning new information I uncovered while writing this, but more because of the place where I am standing. I am using the lens of spiritual, cultural experience, looking more through past-middle-aged eyes and less through the eyes and ears of a social scientist. I am more interested in what Springsteen fans do and what these things do *for* them, and less concerned with *why* they do what they do.

After ten years and 60-some shows, I am now never alone at a concert, never alone in a distant city, never alone anywhere in the world. Fans in cities all over the world have opened their homes, hearts, and lives to me just because I share their love of a man's music, because we have that common bond and frame of reference. In Italy, one fan proudly showed me the room where he kept his Bruce-relics—shelves full of bootleg compact disks, framed pictures and posters on the walls, ticket stubs proudly preserved and lovingly displayed. He and his wife, who met through their mutual love of Bruce, drove us up into the hills above Trieste for lunch at a truly local restaurant, hidden as it was so far up in those hills. This couple had met as a result of trading Bruce bootlegs and married a short time later. Jack and Jane in Northern Ireland hosted my traveling companion (a very, very recent convert to the Church of Bruce) and me for lunch in their charming cottage, introducing us to their three children. I missed meeting Poet in Israel because he'd gone abroad right before I arrived, but I managed to meet up with Calvin and her friends in Cologne, Germany; I experienced and consequently learned about German beer that night, much to my head's detriment! (My other companion that evening was a Bruce-fanfriend from Buffalo, and someone I'd come to see at nearly every show, regardless of country.) We shopped on the coast of Australia in lovely St. Kilda with our hostess Sabrina, who graciously squired us around Melbourne and showed us the theater where Springsteen played on *The Rising* Tour (all tours tend to be named after the album they support). Mel helped us find our way to the Sidney Zoo after bestowing an armful of compact disks on me so we would have music to listen to as we drove around. And the wonderful Ms. S spent two days taking us sightseeing in Auckland while she and I talked about all things Bruce.

When taking account of my Bruce contacts, I cannot forget to mention the cyber communities in which I participate. Some of the people I have conversed with online I have met "in real life" (IRL), and with some I have developed relationships that have become a natural part of my life; I have even acquired a few new extended family members.

Another important thing I discovered through Bruce was the ability to age. To be more precise—he has given me the *courage* and freedom to age. We are age cohorts, Bruce and I, and we will ease into our 60s and "mature" years together. He has provided me with a spiritual template to use in my own life. I am someone who has never adjusted to organized religion, but who longs for something to believe in, something to provide a little warmth on those cold nights of the soul, some "reason to believe." Springsteen has provided illumination for me and for many of his faithful fans in the form of joy, and I am thankful for this. Joy may be the emotion that brings us closest to the holy, and joy is what I feel when seeing Bruce in concert; joy is "getting it."

Religion is not just one thing, as John Caputo says; it is too big to fit under the shelter of one definition, and is "uncontainably diverse" (2001:1). Clifford Geertz says that religion is a cultural system, one whose "sacred symbols function to synthesize a people's ethos . . . its moral and aesthetic style" (1973:89). This is what Bruce Springsteen's music and performance represent to me—a moral landscape that I can negotiate and from which I can derive some spiritual sustenance.

Springsteen fans have—knowingly or unknowingly—created a culture, a web "of significance" (Geertz 1973:5). This book is an ethnography of the inhabitants of Springsteen nation, and a possible explanation for the *whys* of its existence. Geertz says that ethnography is a *doing*, "establishing rapports, selecting informants, transcribing texts" in an attempt to describe, to portray, or to explicate a socially established code; it is "thick description" (1973:6). While I may not have explained the detailed *whys* of certain behaviors I have observed in my fieldwork, I have presented what I see as the genesis of behaviors and customs. But this is not an exact science. Culture—any culture—cannot be quantified and measured exactly—cannot have a guaranteed interpretation or explanation. The following excerpt from *The Interpretation of Cultures* by Clifford Geertz captures the quicksilver that is cultural anthropology:

> In finished anthropological writings . . . this fact—that what we call our data are really our own constructions of other people's constructions of what they and their compatriots are up to—is obscured because most of what we need to comprehend a particular event, ritual, custom, idea, or whatever is insinuated as background information before the thing itself is directly examined . . . [thus,] ethnography is thick description. Doing ethnography is like trying to read a manuscript . . . written not in conventionalized graphs of sound but in transient examples of shaped behavior. (1973:9–10)

My position within the fan culture means that I am reporting from an *emic* position, that of an insider. Anthropology attempts to explain the behavior and thoughts of people/groups, and fieldwork is the way in which information is gathered, with the anthropologist firmly placed within the culture—observing, recording, and interpreting, yet remaining apart. My position as a fan gave me a unique vantage point from which to observe, but it may also have influenced my interpretations. Fieldwork is not a static thing, but rather it is a flow, constantly morphing and changing as people change. An almost poetic explanation of ethnographic fieldwork and its fluidity describes it eloquently: "Anthropologists . . . often return to the field, pick up threads and find themselves weaving a very differently patterned cloth from that which they wove so confidently during their previous encounter" (Watson 1999:1). I have tried to be as objective as possible, but anthropology is never exclusively objective because one can never truly shed preconceptions or closely held beliefs. While I may have been an active participant in Springsteen fan culture and have reported conversations and testimonials along with my observations, there is never any sure way to guarantee that I have gotten it right. Watson uses the example of a smile, a common gesture, to illustrate the possible different ways one can make a wrong assumption about a simple thing; is it a smile of happiness, or a smug smile of triumph? Is it a smile of affection, or does it signify ridicule and disdain? (1999:3). We observe the gesture, report on the situation in which the gesture is made, record the reactions—if any—of those around, and then make a best guess, an interpretation. There are risks involved with anthropologists "going native," becoming too involved with the subjects of their research, especially if there is a power dynamic involved or authority issues. My research, however, holds none of these risks, and so I was never concerned with "going native." Besides, it was too late to worry about this; once I realized that I had a subject ripe for reporting on, I had already gone native.

My data were collected over the course of eleven years, informally and using opportunistic and serendipitous observation and sampling. Opportunistic sampling consists of using the sources available to you at the time, such as people who resemble or fit the loose profile you are seeking—in this case, Springsteen fans. I did not seek out nonfans to see how Springsteen affected them emotionally, as their opinions would not serve my purpose. If you want to know how a hot dog tastes, you don't look for ice cream to eat. I wanted to know how avid fans felt, acted, and reacted, so my contacts were restricted to Springsteen fans, the "real" fans who traveled from show to show, or to those who are denizens of the message boards and Web sites dedicated to all things Springsteen.

As stated previously, I have attended nearly 70 concerts in a multitude of regions and countries, spending countless hours with fans talking about Bruce, and more hours in arenas and stadiums listening to him. My methods were simple—I engaged people in conversations, either in person or via Internet fan sites, wherever I found them. Sometimes, this meant chatting in line at the supermarket or starting a conversation in the lobby of a movie theater because I spotted someone wearing some Springsteen artifact. Attempts at getting fans to fill out questionnaires were for the most part unsuccessful, and I found that I could learn much more by personally asking questions. Some of the fans I spoke with never identified themselves by name, and some names I forgot before I managed to make notes. I chose not to whip out pen and paper during conversations, as the first few times I did this, my conversation partner simply shut down, and all conversation was squashed. Much of my information is anecdotal. Because of the nature of my communications with many fans—via e-mail and Internet bulletin boards—documentation has been awkward in some instances, and impossible to backtrack in others. It is part of cyber life that Web sites (and computers) crash. The largest Internet Springsteen fan site, backstreets.com, crashed several years ago and all posts were lost. Members were forced to reregister, and chaos ensued when screen names used for years were no longer available, and well-known posters were no longer identifiable. Recently, another valuable site, greasylake.org, likewise crashed, and when it came back up, mountains of data were missing. These are not professionally run sites, but rather a work of love and devotion, and there are no guarantees for data security. For this, I offer my apologies for sources that cannot be traced, and URLS that no longer lead anywhere. What I have done is listed all the Internet sites from which I garnered stories and anecdotes in hopes that readers will browse the sites and read for themselves the many stories of other fans.

If culture is, as Geertz (1973) proposes, the psychological structures that determine and guide individual and group behavior, then this community of stalwart and dedicated fans can look to the author of the music that inspires us as the creator of our culture. Bruce Springsteen, in this sense, is the father of our nation, as well as our father who art in Asbury. It is from this perspective that I have approached the subject matter.

Chapter 1

Joining the Church of Bruce and the Ministry of Rock 'n' Roll

May your faith give us faith
May your hope give us hope
("Into the Fire")

Living in Upstate New York in 1999, I was already a card-carrying member of AARP, and far removed from the rockin' 'n' rollin' days of my youth. But one blustery winter's day while walking down Main Street, something caught my eye. The poster in the music store window was advertising tickets for Bruce Springsteen and the E Street Band's first show together in 14 years. Seeing this, I remembered that moment 24 years before when I'd first "discovered" Bruce, as his fans familiarly refer to him. The album was *Born To Run*, and the poetry and imagery had overwhelmed me with its emotion and understanding. But life moves on, and after seeing him in concert once in 1975, I gave little thought to either the man or the music over the course of the next two decades. Life got in the way as it always does, and 30-plus years went by like a fading memory. Still, something pulled at me when I saw this poster, and I decided to buy tickets and go even though I'd long since given up attending rock concerts. I dutifully lined up at the appointed ticket-buying time and waited in line with 30 or so other people that morning to get my two tickets to the show—no mean feat as I later came to realize.

Three months later I found myself in an arena along with many thousands of other fans, with a dawning realization that I was a novice among acolytes. In spite of the fact that Bruce had not toured with this band in 14 years, everyone seemed to know all the songs, participating as a group in a display of hand gestures and verbal call-and-response to the performance. The anthropologically inclined side of me saw this as "interesting," while the emotionally hungry side felt the meaning and emotion in the building. Something was happening here. I was overwhelmed and nearly speechless at Mr. Springsteen's performance, as well as at the lyrical content of his songs. I passed the three hours enthusiastically and then headed home.

I spent some time reflecting about the emotions that the concert evoked within me and came to no real conclusions other than the rather trite "music is the universal language" kind of thing. Sometime shortly after this show, I read that Springsteen and company were playing a show in Charlotte, North Carolina. I had a friend who lived in North Carolina, and so I called her and asked her to get us tickets for the event. She and I went, and again, I experienced a sense of wonder at the amount of emotion that flooded me, emotion that I at first wrote off as contagious enthusiasm. In fact, only one other "public" experience in my life even came close to resembling my Springsteen experience, and that was a Billy Graham crusade I'd attended as a young teen. Springsteen's music and words spoke to me, to some inner longing, as much as Billy Graham's words had some 40 years earlier, and this was both intriguing and mystifying. I have never been a "joiner," never been really passionate about anything. I listened to this man sing:

> I believe in the love that you gave me
> I believe in the faith that can save me
> I believe in the hope
> and I pray that some day
> It may raise me above these badlands, . . .
>
> For the ones who had a notion,
> a notion deep inside
> That it ain't no sin
> to be glad you're alive ("Badlands")

I felt some emotional cog slip into place feeling a part of something bigger than myself, something bigger than that room with 18,000 people in it, but something that included all of us there. How do you put a name to this feeling, to this communion? This man was singing to the audience, not at them; the audience was the "you" in the song. Bruce was singing our shared experiences and emotions, creating a common frame of reference that was inclusive of all of us in the arena. Yes, he told us in song, I have felt that despair, but look! There's hope here too. . . . I found myself suddenly seeing the audience as comrades, fellow travelers on this rocky road called life: "No retreat, baby, no surrender" ("No Surrender"). Without ever having exchanged a word with another fan, I knew we were sharing something meaningful and potent, even if I could not name that feeling.

And I felt just as surely that the man singing on stage was being not only honest and straight, but also completely sincere and earnest. After this show I began to comb the Internet to see what I could find out about the man Bruce Springsteen to verify the impressions I'd felt. I wanted to know why he gave me hope, and if this was something others felt, or if I was suffering from some sort of midlife crisis of faith or possibly simply slipping into early-onset dementia. It was during this process that I began to have some idea of the vastness and depth of the Springsteen community. I discovered Web sites where one could obtain unofficial copies of live concerts ("not for sale—trade only"), get advance notification of ticket sales for shows, buy or sell tickets ("face value only"), discuss my favorite song or the quality of my day, and even find a brownie recipe ("use miniature marshmallows ONLY"). Here were people who were sharing their lives, in varying degrees, with each other on the basis of nothing more tangible than an interest in a musician. I felt as welcome in this community as in any church congregation of which I had ever been a part.

"Come on up for the Rising" ("The Rising"): The Journey Continues

The September 11, 2001, tragedy may eventually claim to be the inspiration for any number of urban myths; Springsteen is the subject of one of those. Legend claims:

> A few days after 11 September, Bruce Springsteen was pulling out of a beach parking lot in the Jersey Shore town of Sea Bright when a fan drove by. The man rolled down his window, shouted "We need you!" and drove on. It was the kind of moment, Springsteen says, that made his career worthwhile. "That's part of my job. It's an honour to find that place in the audience's life." (Guilfoile 2002).

In an interview with Mark Binelli, Bruce comments further on the incident:

> And I thought, well, I've probably been a part of this guy's life for a while, and people wanna see other people they know, they wanna be around

things they're familiar with. So he may need to see me right about now. That made me sense, like, "Oh, I have a job to do." (in Binelli 2002:903)

Shortly after this Sea Bright encounter, Springsteen performed on the fund-raising telethon "A Tribute to Heroes," the first of many benefits held to raise money for the survivors of that day, singing "My City of Ruins," a song about Asbury Park, but eerily appropriate for the occasion.

The album *The Rising* was recorded and released, and Bruce Springsteen and the E Street Band commenced a promotional world tour before the first anniversary of this tragedy. This collection of songs focused not on revenge or blind patriotism but on healing the wounds the 9/11 attacks had left. Also, this release was the first recording of new studio material Springsteen had done with the E Street Band since the 1980s, the first of three albums with the E Street Band over the next seven years. I found out about the tour through the Internet sites I had begun to visit and made plans to again attend the Albany, New York, show. This time, however, I could enlist no one to go with me, and so I went alone. To this point in my life, I had never attended a concert or theatrical performance alone; this was new territory for me. Yet I went, unhesitatingly because I wanted to see if that first rush of emotion and feeling I had felt in Albany and Charlotte would be duplicated, or if it was a fluke; perhaps I'd merely been caught up in the moment, perhaps it was a singular experience not able to be replicated. In the intervening months, I'd come to question what I'd felt, and I needed to test my feelings.

This proved to be a terrific and transforming experience for me. And that is what it truly was—an *experience*—so much more than a rock and roll concert. I felt my initial response of two years ago validated. In some fashion, I felt redeemed and forgiven for all my past bad life- decisions. My response was completely visceral, emotional, nonintellectual, and absolutely unexplainable in the moment. I felt in unison, with all those around me and with myself. This time as the concert ended, I left wanting more, and not at some distant as yet unscheduled time in the future: I wanted it *now.* To feel a part— me, a 53-year-old middle-aged woman—of this joyous, raucous celebration of life, love, friendship, and music was an *extra*ordinary encounter. I experienced transcendence, inclusion, redemption, and felt a part of the performance. I felt the grace of the universe. And then I realized I wanted to know *why* I wanted more, and *why* I felt these decidedly spiritual and emotional waves. I needed to know more, to understand why.

Sitting in the concert hall, I heard and felt a truth and sincerity in the music engulfing me, a truth that touched me in a way no other music or musician had ever done. I am a child of the rock and roll generation; I cut my teeth to Elvis, learned to drive to the Beatles and the Rolling Stones, and had been "saved" by Billy Graham. Twice. What I felt after seeing Springsteen more clearly resembled the raw emotion I'd felt at the Billy Graham crusades I'd attended rather than the multitude of rock and roll shows I'd seen in the course of the past 38 years. I felt this man speaking to my heart, to my life's wins and losses. He identified with my struggles and frustrations, not waiting for me to identify with him, and perhaps that is his talent and genius. Bruce places the onus of understanding on himself, and not the listener; his job is to convince us that he knows what we know, to provide us with hope, and not to ask us to understand him. Sitting there, I felt as surely as I knew my own name that this man needed me as much as I needed him. Later readings verified his absolute acknowledgement of his personal need for audience acceptance and approval, as well as his feelings of insecurity and displacement as an adolescent; but his performance said it all. He was able to articulate all the angst and frustrations of life, while offering the gift that there is always hope: "Dreams will not be thwarted . . . Faith will be rewarded" ("Land of Hope and Dreams"). And I accepted his covenant of faith—"you be true to me / And I'll be true to you" ("Be True")—baptized in the flames of the fiery ministry of rock and roll. My conversion was completed that night; I believed him when he said "Grab your ticket and your suitcase / Thunder's rolling down the tracks" ("Land of Hope and Dreams"). I was now a devout, devoted "Tramp" (how the faithful refer to themselves, taken from the line "'Cause tramps like us, baby we were born to run" from the Springsteen song "Born To Run").

Prior to the Albany concert in December 2002, I knew that one of the Springsteen fan sites—greasylake.org—had planned a get-together before the show, but I had been too apprehensive and anxious to attend. I had actually gotten to the door of the restaurant where the gathering was scheduled to be held and was too afraid to enter. After all, I was already far past the prime rocking and rolling age. I believed that most of the attendees would be decades younger than myself; weren't all people who went to rock concerts 23 at the most? I had noticed older people—my age cohorts—at the shows I'd attended, but I doubted that these were the people haunting the fan sites I'd been reading. Mature adults do not attend rock concerts, befriend each other online, and meet total strangers in restaurants or bars, or so I thought. I decided to find another place to eat and continued down the street, passing up my first opportunity to meet fans from the Internet and the greater Springsteen nation at large.

However, over that winter of 2002–2003 I began to realize that the dimensions of devotion to the Springsteen credo and values did not exclude my peer group but rather embraced all age groups, and perhaps most especially mine because of the shared historical time (after all, we were the same age, Bruce and I). I began reading and posting on several Web sites and cultivated at least an e-relationship with many fans. By the end of *The Rising* Tour,

I had attended several fan-site-organized tailgate get-togethers and met dozens of fans of all ages and geographical locations. These people were from a variety of lifestyles, but almost to a "man" (and yes, the preponderance of fans I met were male, contrary to what might be the popular assumption that most Springsteen fans are women) they were possessed by the same spirit that I was—the spirit cast by a man of conviction, empathy, and intuitive understanding, a blue-collar prophet. These traits seemed contagious, and the fans I met were trying—each in his or her own way—to exercise the emotions and values depicted in Springsteen's songs. At one such gathering of 200–300 fans in August 2003, I managed to collect nearly $3,000 for the Second Harvest Food Bank of New Jersey in less than an hour. Total strangers were shoving fifty-dollar bills into my hand. No one asked for receipts or questioned my motives; for weeks after that, checks kept arriving in the mail. If you were to ask any of these people what made them give this money to a total stranger, the answer would have been something in the vein of "because she's a fan, she wouldn't deceive us" or some similar sentiment. I came to realize over the course of the next several years that this was the norm and not in the least exceptional, and I would in fact see greater acts of charity enacted in Springsteen's honor.

Curious as to why this man and his music could motivate strangers to toss money at me, I began to explore Springsteen's back catalog of songs, reading lyrics and listening to album after album. It is all there in his lyrics, laid naked for the pilgrim to see: concerns about justice and fairness, about friendship and honesty, about rejection and personal revelation, and ultimately, redemption. There is little mystery about Bruce Springsteen, only stark openness that appears to reveal his soul to any and all comers. It would seem that he believes what he writes, and further lives what he believes. For 35-plus years, people have been trying to see "behind" the man, to expose his soft under-belly, and to date no one has. Either he is genuine, or he is the all-time absolute best actor. His fans—and I include myself in that multitude—have decided he is the "real deal." There is no visible dissonance between his stage persona, his private self, and his public self.

What further intrigued me was the way that Springsteen fans referred to the concerts and to their discovery of his music and fan community; the language was that of religion, where fans spoke of "conversions" and "redemption," "epiphanies," and "faith." Concerts are congregations of the faithful gathered in joyous celebration with the Minister of Rock and Roll, Bruce Springsteen. To be clear, not one fan I have ever spoken with has alluded to Springsteen being a deity. Yet, the obvious fact remains that many fans take away from his music and performances much of the feeling and comfort that a traditional worship service offers—by their own assertions. Moreover, the connection that individual fans feel toward each other mirrors the connections members of worship-communities share and is reflected in a number of group activities and actions. The fan community has its own version of church suppers, bazaars, and fund-raisers, and those who cannot personally participate join in virtually, by way of the various Web sites run for and by fans.

With my interest piqued, I began to look at the way rock and roll music is also used by fans in the process of constructing adult identities in teenagers— or perhaps it is more accurate to say it *was* used; each generation develops its own music, and rock and roll belongs to the baby-boomer generation, the post–World War II babies of the fifties and sixties. As Joseph Kotarba says, "The music and musical culture they (baby boomers) grew up with has stayed with them and has become the soundtrack of American culture . . . people who, over the course of their lives, have come to use rock 'n' roll as a source of meaning for their joys and sorrows" (Kotarba 2002:103–104). But this music is no longer the sole province of youth—the youth of today have moved past rock music to embrace hip-hop, techno, emo, rap, and house music as their modes of expression. The baby boomers are not only the first rock and roll generation to age out—we may be the *only* rock and roll generation. Rock music is now for the most part relegated to the "classic rock" radio stations and the VH1-Classic television channel. It is, however, an indelible part of many aging adults' lives, at least in today's Western world culture.

Music has always been used through the ages by people to reconstruct a point in time, to summon up a memory. So the aging baby boomers use rock 'n' roll; to use an overused but accurate cliché, it is the sound track to our lives, the background noise to our joys, disappointments, hopes, and dashed dreams. To have a meaningful artist who has aged with us, remained vital, and not drifted into nostalgia to become a rock caricature tells us that we, too, can still maintain the optimism and vitality of our younger selves. The American Association of Retired People acknowledged the aging rock 'n' roll generation recently by having Bruce Springsteen grace the cover of the September/October 2009 issue of *AARP: The Magazine*, with the headline "The Boss Turns 60." The editor of the magazine, Nancy Perry Graham, is a Springsteen fan and calls her regular column in the publication "E Street"; in the January/February 2010 edition, she talks about wearing a tee shirt with the Springsteen cover art from the issue on it at the October 3, 2009, Giants Stadium Springsteen show.

With the aging of the baby-boomer generation, rock 'n' roll has become a more legitimate topic of academic study; in fact, Liverpool Hope University in England now offers a Master's degree in The Beatles, Popular Music, and Society (hope.ac.uk). The stamp of approval of the academic community signifies a certain authenticity to any course of study, and while there may not be a Springsteen "curriculum" yet, there is already a body of academic literature that has been published about him. Since publications represent intellectual capital for academics, these writings are tangible evidence that Springsteen in particular—and rock 'n' roll in general—has matured to the stage where he—and it—can now receive serious intellectual consideration, accruing intellectual capital and credibility.

The Springsteen Collection at the Asbury Park Library boasts thousands of holdings, including a number of scholarly articles with titles that range from "Radical Traditionalism: The Passion of the Artistic in a Time of Crisis" (Shasha 2006) to "Crime, Lawbreaking, and Counter hegemonic Humanism in Springsteen songs" (Pappke 2006) to "Whitman, Springsteen, and the American Working Class" (Smith 2000). The *Widener Law Journal* dedicated an entire volume of the journal to papers presented during a symposium held in 2005 entitled "The Lawyer as Poet Advocate: Bruce Springsteen and the American Lawyer" (2005). Over 120 lawyers from 17 states and the District of Columbia participated in the symposium, presenting papers on topics ranging from "The Dignity and Humanity of Bruce Springsteen's Criminals" to "The Judgment of the Boss on Bossing the Judges."

That same year, 2005, Penn State University held the first *Glory Days: A Bruce Springsteen Symposium* on the Monmouth University campus in New Jersey. Here, for three days, over 300 academics attended sessions that included diverse topics, such as "The Law According to Springsteen: The Influence of Springsteen's Wisdom and Lyrics on the Judiciary and Legal Scholarship," "The Boss and the Bible," and "How a Chicana Became a Jersey Girl." The man chiefly responsible for this event was Mark Bernhard, director of the Department of Continuing and Professional Education at Virginia Tech University. In a personal e-mail received from SH: "The symposium started with Mark having the idea to develop it when he was at Penn State; he contacted Jerry Zolten and Ken Womack at the Penn State Altoona campus to help him and the three of them created the first symposium."

Bernhard then left Penn State for Virginia Tech and decided to organize the second symposium from there, with Penn State and Monmouth University again being cosponsors (now along with Virginia Tech).

When I asked Bernhard how difficult it was organizing a symposium around a topic as seemingly frivolous as a rock 'n' roll musician, his response was: "I can't say I met a ton of resistance for the event. I did hear a lot of chuckles or people not understanding that this could be a true academic/educational undertaking. I just believed in the vision of the event." (Bernhard). The response was satisfying, with over 300 Springsteen fans from all professions and walks of life gathering at Monmouth University in Monmouth, New Jersey, to study all things Bruce. Over 100 papers were presented by participants from throughout the United States and eight different countries.

The first *Glory Days Symposium* was so successful that a second was held in September 2009, again at Monmouth University. Sponsored by Virginia Tech along with The Pennsylvania State University, this symposium again saw participants from around the globe converging on the campus in Monmouth to analyze and celebrate Bruce Springsteen. "We like to call it an educational gathering. And this is not just academics talking to academics," said Bernhard (Duffy 2009). Presenters and attendees covered the age ranges of 16 to mid-'70s. The nighttime "sessions" took place at the legendary Stone Pony in Asbury Park, in the form of musical performances by artists that had some connection with Springsteen, with even seventy-somethings attending. My field notes from one such session read, "I have never seen so many old men with guitars," and this was an observation referring to the performers, not the audience. Preconference sessions were also held that focused on using Springsteen in the classroom. Regular breakout sessions covered a range of topics, from "The Aging of the E Street Nation" (Dr. D. Bernstein) to sessions on Springsteen's storytelling. Other session titles included: "Springsteen and Gender"; "Springsteen and Law and Order"; "Springsteen and Pedagogy"; "Springsteen and Mortality, Absence and Loss"; "Springsteen and Transcendence"; and "Springsteen and Alienation, Loss and Disability." The General Session Key Note Address, "Springsteen: The Road to Resilience in Hard Times," was co presented by Steven Southwick (professor, Yale University School of Medicine), Linda Godleski (associate professor of psychiatry, Yale University School of Medicine, known to me by a message board screen name), and Dennis Charney (dean, Mount Sinai School of Medicine). The address spoke to Springsteen's ability to lyrically "guide us through the steps of resilience," providing a "supportive environment" for our emotional responses to situational crises, helping us to cope with whatever angst with which we are grappling. All of this gives some indication of the seriousness with which the participants in this symposium approached their subject— Bruce Springsteen, in all his complex and over-analyzed glory.

Other presentations at the conference included the "Springsteen and Social Consciousness" panel discussion, featuring as panelists former World Hunger Year Chair Jen Chapin, who said that Springsteen has donated or helped raise over $8 million for the group: "Bruce's integrity is unmatched. When he says he'll do something, we know he will," said Chapin. Kathleen DiChiarra, president and CEO of the Community Food Bank of New Jersey, told us about a $230,000 check for emergency food shipments to New Orleans after Katrina; Bob Benjamin, the founder of Light of Day Foundation, an organization that supports the fight against Parkinson's Disease, also spoke about Springsteen's involvement in raising funds for that organization. A presentation by Jim Musselman, president of Appleseed Recordings, entitled "We Shall Overcome: Bruce Springsteen's Trip into the Folk Playground," detailed Bruce's connection with and foray into the folk genre, and "Ten Years Burning Down the Road: Bruce Springsteen in the 21st Century," was presented by Lauren Onkey, the vice president of education and public programs at the Rock and Roll Hall of Fame.

All the sessions I attended were scholarly and serious, sincere and passionate, and displayed a level of intensity, interest, and academic dedication rarely afforded a rock musician. As with most academic conferences, the simultaneous presentation of four or more breakout sessions meant that I was able to attend less than 20 percent of the offerings. Said one attendee, "If you are a serious Springsteen fan or someone who takes rock and roll seriously as an avenue for scholarly study, the *Glory Days Symposium* is Mecca" (Duffy 2009).

The last presentation of the 2009 symposium was entitled "Landlordess Redux—1974–2009: Glory Days of a Jersey Girl: Musings and Memories of New Jersey's Most Famous Tenant and the House Where He Wrote 'Born To Run'"—recollections by Springsteen's former landlady (he called her his "landlordess") Marilyn Rocky, the owner of said house. The title of the session is itself a detailed account of what was discussed. A fun ending to an educational and exuberant conference, this session offered little in the way of new insight or information about Bruce Springsteen, but it did add anecdotes to the Springsteen-lore annals; Rocky told a story about the piano that was in the house when Bruce moved in, and on which he subsequently wrote the songs on the *Born To Run* album. This piano remained as part of the permanent furnishings over the years of renters, passed on by default from lessee to lessee. One day, shortly after the closing on the sale of the house, Ms. Rocky ran into E Street Band member Clarence Clemons at her dentist's office. After chatting and reminiscing for a bit, Clarence asked if the piano was still in the house and talked about how each member of the E Street Band had signed their names on the inside of the piano. Realizing the potential value, Ms. Rocky immediately went to the house only to find that the new owners had hauled all the old furnishings, including this priceless piece of rock history, out onto the sidewalk for trash pickup. Rocky said that she attempted to find the piano, visiting several dumps and landfills, but to no avail. Somewhere, this piano sits, waiting to assume its rightful place in Cleveland, at the Rock and Roll Hall of Fame Museum.

Fans as scholars, fans as storytellers, fans as philanthropists—meaning comes in multiple guises for the Springsteen fan community. In the following pages, I illustrate the ways in which Springsteen has sown the seeds for this diverse group and laid the groundwork for this spiritual "home" the fans have created, influenced by his words, music, and deeds. This home works to provide much of the same sort of emotional, social, and spiritual sustenance that traditional worship communities offer, as explained and defined by the fans themselves. By identifying with the persona of Bruce Springsteen and his working-class, ordinary Joe image, fans derive more than entertainment from his performances and music, finding faith and inspiration that serves them in their daily lives. My approach to this subject uses the anthropological notion of an emic perspective because of my own involvement with—and within— the Springsteen community. Much of the information included in this book comes from personal experience and participant-observation, as well as from conversations over the years with members of the fan community and concert audiences. In particular, two Web sites that are representative of the fan community have been invaluable sources of information: greasylake.org and backstreets.com. Fans from all over the world post on these sites that operate as cyber bulletin boards and that serve as the locus for much of the social activity and fund-raising efforts common in the fan community. Using the words of the people involved, I also show the ways in which fan admiration and love have manifested as charitable actions patterned after the real—or assumed—actions of Mr. Bruce Springsteen.

Chapter 2

Releasing Religion

Still at the end of every hard earned day
people find some reason to believe
("Reason to Believe")

"*R*eligion," said Dr. Gregory House, on a recent episode of the currently popular television show *House,* "is a symptom of irrational belief and groundless hope." This fictional persona, House, was attempting to diagnose a patient who had recently converted to Hasidic Judaism; House considered this conversion to be a *symptom* of the patient's undiagnosed condition, and therefore of diagnostic significance rather than spiritual importance (as it turns out, there was no connection between her conversion and her disease). As on this show, religion comes at us through all mediums these days, whether in the form of fictionalized characters on a TV drama, Christian rock on the radio, or televangelists attempting to save our souls; it is everywhere. And just as we are assaulted with any number and kinds of religious messages daily, so are we confronted with multiple concepts of what religion *is,* as well as what it can do.

Clifford Geertz says that religion is a set of symbols that "establish powerful, pervasive, and long lasting moods and motivations" (in Pals 2006:270) and that offer an ultimate explanation of the world. Durkheim says these symbols unite us into "moral communities" where we are concerned not simply with our individual well-being but also with the welfare of the group (Pals 2006:96). In these days of appliances built-for-one—single-cup coffee makers—solitary Internet communication, and rabid individualism, many people search for that "moral community" and sense of belonging that brings extra meaning and dimension to our lives. Our moral communities provide us with a common belief system shared by members, common frames of reference, and a set of moral ground rules by which to live our lives. The (institutionalized) church—regardless of religion or denomination—is no longer the sole proprietor of this territory—if it ever was—as many people seek far and wide for some reason to believe, and some place to belong. Various people, it seems, are either replacing traditional religion or are adding other resources to supplement their traditional religious beliefs. Many Americans no longer look first to the church for direction in their lives, and the church has also diminished as a source of sociality and community. Participation in church activities outside of worship services has decreased by 50 percent since the 1950s (Putnam 2000:72). In the twenty-first century, what theologies, products, and forms will offer us solace and spiritual nourishment and a sense of community or belonging to something bigger than ourselves? What will inspire and challenge us to become better people?

As institutionalized religious practices become more polarized and polarizing, many people find themselves unfulfilled by conventional religious services and rituals. Organized religion has become more, well, *organized*. Gordon Lynch (2004) says that formal religion has diminished as a source of comfort and inspiration for many people, and for some, music has stepped in to fill the gaps. According to a recent survey conducted by the Pew Forum on Religion and Public Life (2008), mainline Protestant churches are suffering dwindling congregations, and more people are declaring themselves "unaffiliated." Church attendance is falling, as is participation in the rites and rituals associated with religion such as christenings, baptisms, and church weddings. And this loss is not restricted to Christianity; synagogues and mosques (in non-Muslim-majority countries) are also suffering (Lynch 2004). More than 25 percent of the people surveyed by the Pew Forum have left the faith of their family of origin, while 25 percent of the adults aged 18–29 deny any religious affiliation at all; among the age group that includes most Springsteen fans, ages 30–49, fully 40 percent claim no religious affiliation (Pew Forum 2008). This might help account for the spiritual identification many fans have with the music; there is no need to worry about conflicts with church dogma or policies if there is no church. But to claim no religious affiliation is not the same as claiming no spirituality.

Additionally, the areas of heaviest fan population in the United States—the states of Massachusetts, Pennsylvania, New York, New Jersey, Maryland, and Virginia—correspond geographically with those polled who self-identified as unaffiliated (Pew Forum 2008). This information is submitted anecdotally, and in no way implies that all Northeast corridor residents claiming no religious affiliation are Bruce Springsteen fans, or the reverse. (Springsteen's core audience initially was cultivated in the bars and clubs on a circuit that extended from Asbury Park north through Boston, and south through the beach towns of Virginia; when he began recording, it was the radio stations in these areas that were responsible for the bulk of the airplay he initially received.) However, the information/statistics are suggestive.

There also may be some connection between the lack of official church association and the large number of Springsteen fans in Europe, where secularization has been the rule rather than the exception—what *Religion and Ethics Weekly* refers to as "Europe's long and dramatic decline in church attendance" (see Lynch 2006:481–488). As Lynch says, "alternative spiritualities are providing social spaces and cultural resources for religious affiliation, identities, and meaning-construction beyond the walls of the church, synagogue, or mosque" (Lynch 2006:482). This alternative spirituality carries its congregants into the concert hall and to the "ministry" of Bruce.

The Encyclopedia Britannica online defines the term *congregation* as "an assembly of persons, especially a body assembled for religious worship or habitually attending a particular church. . . . As it is used in the Old Testament, congregation sometimes refers to the entire Israelite community, and at other times it means a gathering or assembly of people." Springsteen nation certainly falls within these parameters, as each concert is a gathering of the faithful, a celebration of our culture and our "religion." If one uses Durkheim's explanation of moral communities cited previously, where concern focuses on the welfare of the group rather than the welfare of the individual, the fan community fits here as well. One way this concern manifests is in the bestowing of tickets—"faerieing" as fans refer to it—on those people who either were unable to get a ticket when they went on sale or were unable to afford a ticket. Fans routinely leave preshow gatherings and meet-ups with a heart-felt "have a good show." Springsteen fans also take care of their own, collecting funds for memorial donations or flowers when a loved-one of some fan has died or providing a fan in need with whatever the community can supply, be it cat food, dollars, or gifts. The fan community so much resembles a religious community that a friend (who is not a fan) observed that people outside of the fan community talk about Springsteen fans "like you'd talk about Scientologists"—with amusement and deprecation. He further says, "anyone who is not a Springsteen fan knows what you mean when you say 'she's a Springsteen fan.'" (When I begin to talk Springsteen, this friend immediately assumes an amused look on his face and laughs if I try to make a cogent point. Not everyone can be converted.)

"And I'm Just Out Here Searchin'
For My Own Piece of the Cross"
("I'll Work For Your Love")

To ferret out the meaning individuals derive from anything in their lives it becomes necessary to focus on action and active involvement. Gordon Lynch states, "It is inadequate to make inferences about the values and beliefs of Western culture simply through studying popular culture 'texts'" (2004:164). People tend to take the information that they need to make a decision or to find personal "meaning" and make it work for them. This interpretation of "meaning" cannot be controlled by the producer of the resource used or manipulated to "give" meaning; instead, the meaning may be translated differently (decoded) and independently, depending on each consumer's own individual circumstance and taste—through a personal lens (Lynch 2004). Stuart Hall calls the delivery system by which this information is received—and used effectively in popular culture—as "encoding" (Lynch 2004:163). Information is presented in such a way as to extract a particular response or interpretation. But during the "decoding" process, the "audience" or receptors (consumers) decode the information in a manner that best suits them, sometimes creating different meanings than those initially intended, meanings that are situationally dependent (Lynch 2004). In simpler terms, "meaning" can be situational, changing as context changes. Here is where individuals determine what is meaningful for them, based on their own personal needs. It is not useful, therefore, to try to interpret these encoded messages without observing the specific situation within which the message is delivered and where the people involved decode it for themselves. Herein lay the value of participant observation and conversation, where one can have the opportunity to *qualitatively* describe the whys and hows of individuals' actions and beliefs based on context, *their* context and not one that has been externally imposed.

Until fairly recently, the domain of assigning appropriate labels to cultural/spiritual rites and customs has resided in the academy (Chidester 1996). Academics and scholars have told us what is and what is not a "real" religion, what constitutes a new religious movement, and what is simply social practice and custom. They are ultimately embroiled in an ongoing crusade to affix meaning, something akin to bottling lightening, and to tame it into an immutable force. Meaning, for many scholars, must be fixed and static to be valid, and not situationally interpreted as discussed previously; symbols must represent the same idea or value whenever seen. Other outside attempts to identify practices and belief systems as religion have been ridiculed and dismissed out of hand (Chidester 1996). Many of the new religious movements have been called "cults" and denied the status of religion in name, in respect accorded, and in tax status. Instead, they have been labeled as "entrepreneurial businesses, politically subversive movements, or coercive, mind-controlling, and brain-washing 'cults'" (Chidester 1996:760). The ordinary men and women who feel something outside the parameters of proscribed "official" religion in unorthodox settings have no way—and apparently no authority—to determine or even translate the spirituality of these feelings for themselves.

However, recent scholarship and the wealth of popular culture have challenged this narrow definition of religion. Popular culture—"that which is (or has been) accepted or approved of by large groups of people" (Forbes 2000:4)—can be a conduit into another world (Albanese 1999), a world where we can explore meanings and meaningfulness for ourselves. In these other worlds, we can experience a place of transcendence from the trials and travails of ordinary life. Popular culture can provide a platform on which our definitions of religion can be allowed to expand and grow to accommodate new ways of "believing." Cultural religion reflects our search for religious and spiritual experience and our need for a feeling of community based on mutual involvement in something beyond the traditional definition of religion, as well as our need and right to define "religion" for ourselves (Albanese 1999). Common grace "subverts preconceived notions" of who gets to broker the relationship between the divine and ourselves—who gets to speak for the divine—and makes spirituality/God "bigger" (Detweiler and Taylor 2003:16–17). Seekers chart their own way across this landscape, searching for that transcendent moment, that feeling of connection and inclusion, that "one face / that ain't looking through me" ("Badlands").

David Chidester (1996) proposes that religion be classified as an activity that is organized and that functions as traditional churches do. In this rendering, religion is symbols and systems of symbols that are sacred, and that imbue the world with value for the "believers" who utilize these symbols. Chidester maintains that the explication of religion is "constantly at stake in the interchanges of cultural discourses and practices" (1996:745), an attribute that keeps it vital and growing. Chidester's (1996) analysis of baseball as religion provides us with a good, working model for identifying the Springsteen fan community as a "congregation," using this skeletal framework of *continuity, uniformity, sacred space,* and *sacred time.*

Looking through this lens, *continuity* is maintained by Springsteen's 35-plus-year career of thoughtful lyrics and public appearances. Steadfastness of viewpoint and delivery, as well as personal civic activity, has created a model of ideals over time, with his blue-collar/everyman persona cementing his position as bard of the working class. A large segment of Springsteen's audience has been attending his shows for most of these 35 years, and the sharing of memories of these shows with other, younger fans helps maintain the legacy and myths that surround Springsteen. *Uniformity* and a sense of belonging emanate from the mutual admiration for Mr. Springsteen and from the fans' attendance at shows. Fans know that they are in the company of other acolytes, and trust is established (to varying degrees) around this fact; the concert hall or stadium becomes a place filled with like-minded individuals—"tramps" all—joined in mutual admiration and trust. The concert spot itself represents the *sacred space* similar to one's customary place of worship, a place where all "believers" are welcome. This is also the spot of *sacred time* and ritual, where "congregants" can celebrate the music itself as well as celebrate *in* the music. To a lesser extent, this sense of "home" can be derived from recordings, but the real celebration of faith takes place in the concert hall. In traditional organized religion, it is possible for one to sit home and read religious texts rather than attend a worship service, but the true sense of being part of a religious community requires attendance at a service or function where fellow believers congregate, participating in the rites and rituals that attend that particular religion.

In the Springsteen fan community, congregants—"true believers"—travel from city to city, attending and participating in as many "services" as possible. Just as outsiders unfamiliar with the rituals and responses required of congregants at, say, a Catholic worship service may be confounded by the mass, so are many outsiders or nonfans confounded by the activities of the audience during a show. Their performed "rituals"—the pumping of fists during "Badlands" or the chorus of oh-oh-oh-oh-ohs sung only by the audience during the same song, the audience singing the first verse of "Hungry Heart" before the band chimes in—help define and delineate "believer" from nonbeliever, affirming and reinforcing the "social solidarity of a community . . . meeting personal needs and reinforcing social integration" (Chidester 1996:748). (Not coincidentally, in this same article, Chidester also speaks about the "inherently religious character of rock 'n' roll" [1996:753].)

Ritual takes many forms. The dictionary definitions include a "prescribed form of a ceremony; a ceremonial act, and; a customary or regular procedure" (*American Heritage Dictionary* 2001:720). Worship services abound in variety and kinds of ritual, depending on the religion. In a Christian worship service, the group recitation of particular passages, the singing of hymns, the taking of communion, and even having coffee after the service are rituals and rites whose meanings are understood by the congregation. However, a Methodist congregation member might be mystified by a Unitarian coffee hour after the worship service and the function it serves (for current members to bond and for visitors and new members to converse with long-standing members of the church). As a child, I recall going to Catholic mass with friends and being utterly perplexed by the kneeling and the burning of incense. Christian Science services are a far cry from a Baptist prayer meeting, and all of these Christian denominations mentioned differ vastly from other non-Christian religious traditions.

Popular music, in the guise of rock and roll, and its inherent attitude of *dis*-organization and looming chaos, has presented some seekers with a replacement or supplement to the community once found through religion: Bruce Springsteen and the devoted fan community that surrounds him. In many ways this community now serves to function as both a social network and a spiritual community—much as the organized church has in the past—offering belonging and support as well as presenting a vehicle for doing "good works." For numerous fans, the music and concert events along with preconcert gatherings offer the same support, relief, release, and connection that traditional worship services offer their congregations. "Belief systems always rest upon a social base . . . and in modern society the social structures" underpinning commitment have moved away from the society at large to smaller units of shared experience (Roof 1978:52). As the church once did, and still does for some, the music, person, and concert experience of the audience at a Bruce Springsteen concert offers transformation and transcendence through the "majesty, the ministry of rock and roll" (Springsteen in concert). These are hard things to talk about—the genesis of feelings, the origins of emotion and faith—but they cannot be invalidated because there is no scientific measure of meaning, no "big-bang" theory of origin. If this were truly the case, no one could ever meaningfully discuss faith.

Rock and roll, as any music devotee knows, had its beginnings in the gospel music heard in churches mixed with a little rhythm and blues, a dollop of jazz, a splash of country and western, and a heavy influence of African American culture. "Rockin'" is a term that could as easily refer to spiritual rapture as to music and its physicality. Music has always been a vehicle for transporting oneself out of the ordinary into the *extra*ordinary, with words, music, and rhythm weaving together to create an oasis "where time and history" are put on hold (Albanese 1999). Music helps us pay attention to the difficult "questions and concerns of human existence," to make meaning out of a meaningless world. We use music not necessarily in a conscious and deliberately spiritual way, but we nevertheless use it to deal with issues of ultimate concern (Pinn 2003). Here in this "other world" there is a sense of what Catherine Albanese (1999:494) calls "instant community" similar to an evangelical revival, where strangers become friends bonding over a mutually and similarly experienced event. For my purpose here, this description encompasses the Springsteen fan community.

Rock 'n' roll can also function as a tool to teach religious beliefs and values and is increasingly melded into Protestant and Catholic liturgy (Kotarba 2002:122). Many churches offer special services for their congregations that take a more contemporary form targeted at the younger church members, often using rock combos to deliver the musical component of the service. I live in a town with two colleges, and the local Catholic church has one service targeted toward students and young people, featuring guitars and other musical instruments not normally associated with mass. In the winter of 2007, while living in Winston-Salem, North Carolina, I attended a "U2-charist" at a local Episcopal church, a communion service crafted using the music and lyrics of the rock band U2. And in April 2008, a Methodist church in Greensboro conducted services during the month of April around the songs of Bruce Springsteen. A series of four sermons and services, each revolved around one specific Springsteen song. I was able to attend the first of these services, the Hungry Heart Sunday. The 9:00 AM service featured the "worship band" Agents of Grace, while the 11:00 AM service had the chancel choir singing "Hungry Heart." The church bulletin for Sunday, April 6, 2008, explained *why* a sermon series on Springsteen: first, Bruce Springsteen was appearing at the Greensboro Coliseum that month; second, because like many of his parishioners, the minister was a huge Springsteen fan; and third, because for over 30 years, Springsteen's music described the human condition. The featured song was used to "describe struggles we all have as human beings. Then we'll explore what our faith has to say about dealing with those struggles" (Pastor Morris, personal communication 4/06/08). Not surprisingly, the reverend was a longtime fan and devotee of Bruce's music. And more recently, the Trinity Episcopal Cathedral conducted "Sky of Mercy: A Bruce Springsteen Eucharist to Feed Portland's Hungry" in March 2010.

Reverend Suzanne Meyer, a Unitarian Universalist minister, responded to an inquiry from me with her sermon "The Gospel According to Bruce." Reverend Meyer explains that the word "gospel" means good news, and that

> time and again those who have proclaimed good news to the poor and freedom to the captive, have been outsiders, at odds with the religious establishment. . . . The author of a new Gospel is anyone who has the courage and conviction to step out of the crowd and speak the truth: times are bad, people are hurting, honest men and women can't get ahead. But, brothers, sisters we are not helpless or hopeless, there is a better way. And lo and behold, the people hear that good news . . . it resonates within their souls . . . enables them to see that they are not powerless cogs . . . pawns or puppets. This Gospel is not about pie in the sky when you die, but rather this good news enables people to see beyond themselves into a future that holds real promise. (personal communication 1/21/08)

Given this, the analysis of rock 'n' roll as religion is a natural, but why Bruce Springsteen? Why are legions of fans the world over so dedicated and devoted to this particular musician? His music and lyrics are meaningful, his imagery vivid, and his stage show is decidedly that—a stage performance part Broadway, part carnival, part down-home gospel tent revival; yet even the trite and cheesy parts delight and engage the fans, as some part of Mr. Springsteen shines through. His sincerity is never in doubt by his "followers."

Terry Mattingly says that people are now more likely to be exposed to new religious doctrine at the movies or the mall (2005:xxi). Entertainment in the form of movies, television shows, music, magazines, comic books, and of course the Internet now are the largest and most "influential theological training system in the world" (Barna and Hatch 2003:188). In this light, it is no surprise that a rock musician should hold so many in his thrall.

"We'll Let Blood Build a Bridge over Mountains Draped in Stars" ("Worlds Apart")

Springsteen's appeal has roots in his lyrical history of visible integrity, empathy, understanding, and compassion—as well as his perceived personal sincerity and genuineness. Of no little contribution to his *persona* is his history of quietly contributing to charities and causes that dates back some 25-plus years. In the fashion of effective organizations, not unlike religious outreach associations and missions, Springsteen has allocated funds for food banks working with the unemployed, workers' unions, and organizations that provide home repairs for the needy (Walker 2008). At his shows beginning in 1984, and continuing into the present, he has invited local food banks and other charitable organizations to set up collections in the arenas and stadiums where he plays; at each show, he will make a plea from the stage for attendees to consider contributing and working with these organizations to help facilitate change. ("In the end, nobody wins unless everybody wins" is an oft-quoted phrase repeated at shows during the *Born in the U.S.A.* Tour that exemplifies how fans see him.) Usually, there is a song dedicated to these workers on what Springsteen calls "the front lines." These are not the glamorous causes of the celebrity world, or the Hollywood-touted disease du jour foundations, but rather they are the low-profile, gritty organizations trying to help the hardworking man and woman, the migrant farm hand, the laid-off worker, the disenfranchised, the people on the margins of society. In his own words: "I want to try and just work more directly with people; try to find some way to tie into the communities we come into" (in Walker 2008). His concern for social justice for those least represented and/or able to advocate for themselves is obvious and reminiscent of many of the finest past spiritual and community leaders. Part of his appeal to his fans is this "everyman" persona, his concern for the plight of the working, struggling American, where his sincerity and genuineness seem almost palpable.

While this common-man persona that Bruce projects may be part public relations fabrication, his facade has not slipped during his 35 years in the spotlight under the scrutiny of an ever-increasingly cynical public and media. His steadfastness of ideals and his consistent actions support the persona his fans see, and they respect as well as revere Bruce. He is continually heralded as being one of us, a man who knows and remembers his origins and roots. In reading hundreds of accounts of encounters with the man, I have seen no negative responses, heard no story of rudeness or even the ordinary day-to-day unpleasantness that even the best of us can sometimes exhibit. He is a 60-year-old man who grew up in the sixties, can rock out for three-plus hours a show, and has never been suspected of drug use. Most fans respect his privacy when he is with his family, and the lore has it that citizens of his hometown territory in New Jersey are fiercely protective of his privacy. To better understand how his fans come to this place, it becomes necessary to know more about Bruce Springsteen and the forces that helped shape the man he has become.

Chapter 3

Genesis

In the Beginning, There Was Freehold

I come from down in the valley
where mister when you're young
They bring you up to do like your daddy done
("The River")

To understand a person—and the people who hold him or her in esteem—it is necessary to know the texture, the fabric, of his or her life, the emotional warp and woof that results in the finished cloth. Bruce Frederick Springsteen was born September 23, 1949, to working-class parents of Dutch, Irish, and Italian ancestry, and raised in Freehold, New Jersey. The section of town where his family resided was lower-middle-working class, and his neighborhood, known as "Texas" because of the large number of southerners who had migrated there, was on the proverbial wrong side of the tracks (Marsh 2004:24). His childhood and adolescence were outwardly unremarkable. Mom Adele worked as a secretary and Dad Douglas filled any number of different jobs including bus driver, prison guard, and mill worker; the family lived for many years with one or the other set of grandparents during times of financial difficulty. The oldest child, Bruce has two sisters, Pamela and Virginia. Life in blue-collar New Jersey was not easy for the family, with Douglas moving from job to job, and the tension and frustration the elder Mr. Springsteen carried with him influenced his son in ways that would manifest years later in song and story on stage, in a public exorcism and attempt to understand and make sense of his parents' experiences. In Springsteen's own words:

> There was a promise of a right to a decent life, that you didn't have to live and die like my old man did. (in Smith 2002:135)

> When I was really young, I don't remember thinkin' about it much. But as I got older, I watched my father . . . how he would come home from work and just sit in the kitchen all night. Like there was somethin' dyin' inside of him, or like he'd never had a chance to live . . . until I started to feel there was somethin' dyin' inside of me. (in Marsh 2004:319)

In blue-collar New Jersey, the ways out were usually the Garden State Parkway or the New Jersey Turnpike. And as New Jersey plants closed down and industry moved out, the romance and promise of leaving grew into a darker reality. Small wonder Springsteen's work would always be responsive to the social climate of the working class; we write what we know. Years later, when inducted into the Rock and Roll Hall of Fame, he would admit to the audience that the working-man's clothes he wore in concert was his way of honoring his father (Sawyer 2004:2).

Bruce relates that he did not really start living until he "found" music in the form of rock and roll. In his own words: "I lived half of my first 13 years in a trance. I was thinking of things, but I was always on the outside looking in" (in Sandford 1999:15). "The only thing that kept me from giving up when I was young was in the rock 'n' roll music I heard—that there was a meaning in life, a meaning in living" (in Smith 2002:135). This belief in a "meaningful life" will continue to echo throughout his career. In one concert tale often told early in his career, Bruce tells the story of a nun at St. Rose of Lima elementary school stuffing him into a trash can under her desk because that is where, she said, he belonged. This story reveals that Springsteen's feelings of separateness and alienation formed early in his childhood and that they have remained vivid. At the age of seven, Bruce saw Elvis Presley on the *Ed Sullivan Show* and decided to become a musician. Said Springsteen, "I couldn't imagine anyone not wanting to be Elvis Presley." As every Springsteen disciple knows, his mother Adele took out a loan to buy a teenaged Bruce a guitar, an act memorialized in the Springsteen song "The Wish":

> Dirty old street all slushed up in the rain and snow
> Little boy and his ma shivering outside a rundown music store window
> That night on top of a Christmas tree shines one beautiful star
> And lying underneath a brand-new Japanese guitar
>
> I remember in the morning, ma, hearing your alarm clock ring
> I'd lie in bed and listen to you gettin' ready for work

The sound of your makeup case on the sink
And the ladies at the office, all lipstick, perfume and rustlin' skirts
And how proud and happy you always looked walking home
from work

If pa's eyes were windows into a world so deadly and true
You couldn't stop me from looking but you kept me from crawlin'
through
And if it's a funny old world, mama, where a little boy's wishes
come true
Well I got a few in my pocket and a special one just for you

It ain't no phone call on Sunday, flowers or a mother's day card
It ain't no house on a hill with a garden and a nice little yard
I got my hot rod down on Bond Street, I'm older but you'll know
me in a glance
We'll find us a little rock 'n roll bar and baby we'll go out and dance

Well it was me in my Beatle boots, you in pink curlers and mata-
dor pants
Pullin' me up off the couch to do the twist for my uncles and aunts
Well I found a girl of my own now, ma, I popped the question on
your birthday
She stood waiting on the front porch while you were telling me to
get out there
And say what it was that I had to say

Last night we all sat around laughing at the things that guitar
brought us
And I laid awake thinking 'bout the other things it's brought us
Well tonight I'm takin' requests here in the kitchen
This one's for you, ma, let me come right out and say it
It's overdue, but baby, if you're looking for a sad song, well I ain't
gonna play it.

These decidedly unrock-like lyrics give some glimpse into the attraction
his music will eventually offer many millions of fans the world over. After
all, how many other popular musicians have written songs of gratitude to
their mothers? The lyrics of the above song indicate the debt and love that
Springsteen obviously feels for his mother. He credits her with saving him
from his father's life, from keeping him from "crawling through" into that
dead world of limited possibilities and abandoned hope. His mother opened
up the possibility of a world of freedom and release, symbolized in that guitar. But, he tells her in this song, he hasn't changed. "I'm older but you'll

know me in a glance." Adele Springsteen had an obvious impact on her son's view of the working life as something in which to take pride.

His relationship with his father however was tense and difficult, as the elder Springsteen had no understanding or tolerance initially for his son's musical aspirations. Family and life conflicts became the fodder of onstage stories; the Springsteen-lore is replete with many of these concert stories of paternal conflict preceding certain songs.

> I used to always have to go back home. And I'd stand there in that driveway, afraid to go in the house, and I could see the screen door, I could see the light of my pop's cigarette. And I remember I just couldn't wait until I was old enough to take him out once. I used to slick my hair back real tight so he couldn't tell how long it was getting. And try to sneak through the kitchen. But the old man he'd catch me every night and he'd drag me back into the kitchen . . . we'd start talkin' about nothin' much. How I was doin'. Pretty soon he'd ask me what I thought I was doin' with myself, and we'd always end up screamin' at each other. My mother she'd always end up runnin' in from the front room, cryin' and tryin' to pull him off me, try to keep us from fightin' with each other. And I'd always, I'd always end up runnin' out the back door . . . tellin' him how it was my life and I was gonna do what I wanted to do. (in Marsh 2004:25–26)

It was at this point that Bruce would launch into the song "It's My Life" (Atkins and D'Errico 1965)—not one he'd written, but one with which he obviously emotionally identified.

A male friend once told me that if you wanted to make a grown man cry, just ask him about his father. Bruce clearly carried around many conflicting feelings about his own father and what sort of role he played in his life, and again, this is one of the things that fans can relate to—the conflicts with and within our families, and the cascade and range of emotions we can experience when dealing with them. Bruce also talked about his father's referring to "that goddamned guitar." (Since his father's death in 1998, these stories have migrated into the oral history, preserved on bootleg recordings, and are no longer used by him in his performances.) One frequently told tale was that of Bruce's convalescing from a motorcycle accident at home, and his father paying a barber to come to the house to cut Bruce's unruly long hair. Yet when Bruce was rejected by the Selective Service Board and classified 4-F in the late sixties, Douglas Springsteen's reaction was a quiet but heartfelt "Good." This was, after all, in 1968, and the Vietnam War with its military draft posed a reality for teenage boys that the Iraq War does not for today's youth. By telling this story, Springsteen was releasing any resentment toward his father and acknowledging that Douglas was not the uncaring father the previous story may have depicted him as. And by doing this in performance, he provided an example for men in the audience who perhaps had their own father issues. Forgiveness releases us from the bonds of the past.

Despite circumstances that could have made another young man bitter and mean, Bruce Springsteen showed a level of understanding, empathy, and compassion toward his father as they both aged and matured. The 1980 album *The River* included the song "Independence Day" that illustrated his capacity for empathy and forgiveness.

> Well, Papa go to bed now it's getting late
> Nothing we can say can change anything now
> I'll be leavin' in the morning from St. Mary's Gate
> We wouldn't change this thing even if we could somehow
>
> Cause the darkness of this house has got the best of us
> There's a darkness in this town that's got us too
> But they can't touch me now
> And you can't touch me now
> They ain't gonna do to me
> What I watched them do to you
>
> Now I don't know what it always was with us
> We chose the words, and yeah, we drew the lines
> There was just no way this house could hold the two of us
> I guess that we were just too much of the same kind . . .

These are not the words of a grudge-holding, rebelling adolescent, but an understanding adult, and the sort of lyrics on which Springsteen's emotional legacy is built. There is an understanding in this song of the forces that pluck at us over which we have no control, and in spite of the outcome, we can change only how we deal with these forces. Our responsibility is in the way we manage and react to situations that we have no control over. This song is also a public forgiveness of his father, as well as an apology to Douglas Springsteen: "I guess that we were just too much of the same kind." Springsteen's words come from situations understood—even if not experienced—and this empathy pours out in his music; his songs show a remarkable ability to understand whatever situation he is writing about, whether it is an illegal immigrant working in a methamphetamine lab or a Vietnam veteran seeking work. We are accustomed to hearing songs of love and moon and teenaged angst from other musicians, but Springsteen's lyrics mine the deeper emotional waters of single mothers and desolate souls searching for a little peace and happiness, walking on the beaches looking for hope. The creatures and characters in Bruce's songs are men and women with *debts no honest man can pay,* roaming the *Backstreets,* looking for love and action and deals going down—at least on Springsteen's earlier albums. As the years passed, these same characters became tangled up in relationships, lost jobs, gave up hope, and embraced despair only to find redemption in the sublime ordinariness of their lives.

Many of Bruce's songs sound potentially autobiographical, and indeed there must be a component of *self* in any good writing. But Springsteen disavows literal historiography saying "the songs are not literally autobiographical but in some way they're emotionally autobiographical" (Primeaux 1996:8). However, in his book *Songs*, Springsteen admits to some actual history, telling the reader that "I often wrote from a child's point of view: 'Mansion on the Hill,' 'Used Cars,' 'My Father's House'—these are all stories that came directly out of my experience with my family" (2003:138). In concert, Springsteen told the story of an old family car that didn't have reverse gear; his father would park the car on a hill to make it easier to start driving. The words to "Used Cars" reflect more than mere auto-frustration:

> My little sister's in the front seat with an ice cream cone
> My ma's in the backseat sittin' all alone
> As my pa steers her slow out of the lot for a test drive down Michigan Avenue
>
> Now, my ma, she fingers her wedding band
> And watches the salesman stare at my old man's hands
> He's tellin' us 'bout the break he'd give us if he could, but he just can't
> Well if I could, I swear I know just what I'd do
> Now mister, the day the lottery I win I ain't ever gonna ride in no used car again
>
> Now, the neighbors come from near and far
> As we pull up in our brand-new used car
> I wish he'd just hit the gas and let out a cry and tell 'em all they can kiss our asses goodbye
>
> My dad, he sweats the same job from mornin' to morn
> Me, I walk home on the same dirty streets where I was born
> Up the block I can hear my little sister in the front seat blowin' that horn
> The sounds echo all down Michigan Avenue
> Now, mister, the day my number comes in I ain't ever gonna ride in no used car again

It is lyrics in this vein, of the songs quoted above, that give the public a window into Springsteen's childhood and the forces that helped shape the man he has become. The examples are there for the world to read/hear/see and have been analyzed and dissected by pop writers and scholars alike. Fans have heard his music and recognized the humanity of the writer, felt his compassion via his music, and judged him accordingly. They feel connected to this man who most have never and will never meet, but who nevertheless is as familiar as a lover. (The bibliography at the end of this book is only a fraction of the writings available on Springsteen.)

Fans know their history—the Springsteen creation myth, if you will. When the elder Springsteens took their life's savings and moved from their home in Freehold, New Jersey, to California in 1969, 19-year-old Bruce decided to remain in New Jersey—pursuing his music, moving to the shore community of Asbury Park. And it is here in Asbury Park where the "legend" really begins to take shape. Springsteen's name has come to be inextricably intertwined with that of Asbury Park, New Jersey, a seedy little seaside town on the Jersey shore immortalized on his first album *Greetings from Asbury Park*. Asbury at the time—and perhaps presently—suffered from run-of-the-mill political corruption, and funds targeted for urban development never manifested in change for the city. As subject to racial conflict as the rest of late-sixties and early-seventies urban America, July 1970 saw race riots in Asbury Park. There nevertheless was a flourishing music scene that included any number of bands, one of which was Bruce Springsteen's, in whatever the moment revealed: The Castiles, Earth, Child, Dr. Zoom and the Sonic Boom, Steel Mill, and the Bruce Springsteen Band to name some incarnations of his bands. It was an "era of shared apartments and skimpy meals" (Cross 1989:26).

The legendary record executive John Hammond signed Springsteen to a recording contract with Columbia Records in 1972 and released *Greetings from Asbury Park* in 1973. In May of 1974, rock critic Jon Landau of Boston's *Real Paper* was present at a Springsteen performance at the Harvard Theater and wrote the prescient, legendary "I have seen the future of rock and roll and its name is Bruce Springsteen" review (www.massmoments.org). Springsteen's live performances, the furnace where he forged his connection to his audience through both his musical outreach and his active attempts to involve them, were becoming legendary, and his fans many and loyal. Somehow, his absolute sincerity cut through any rock 'n' roll pretenses and touched those who saw him perform.

But it was with the release of his third album, the critically acclaimed *Born To Run*, that the rest of the country and the world began to hear the name Bruce Springsteen, and his nickname, "the Boss." Both *Newsweek* and *Time* featured his face on the cover of their respective magazines the same week in 1975. Springsteen and his music had become ubiquitous, so much so that during his first visit and performances in London, Springsteen rebelled and tore down posters promoting his concert there. Again, these are the unlikely actions of a future rock-icon, but they are indicative of the kind of man and performer Bruce was and still is. In his words, "I wasn't interested in immediate success or how much each particular record sold. I was interested in becoming part of people's lives and, hopefully, growing up with them—growing up together" (Sawyer 2004:1). Instinctively, fans feel this. And now, a leg has been added to this journey that Bruce and his fans are on together; as mortality raises its ugly head, we are now—fan and Bruce—living and dying together. Bruce lost good friend Terry Magovern in July 2007 and longtime band mate Danny Federici in April 2008; a cousin and assistant tour manager died in November 2009 also. Even as those around Springsteen succumb to mortality, the fan community mirrors these events, with several fans active on the message boards dying over the past year, and several more stricken with life-threatening illnesses As Jim Morrison said, no one here gets out alive.

Springsteen's live shows, constructed as if made from fire and heart, continued to create a loyal following, and his fame grew quickly. The ferocity and zeal with which he performed as well as the prolonged performances of three, four, even four-and-a-half hours became the stuff of legends. Because of contractual and legal issues, however (he had fired and brought suit against his manager Mike Appel during the recording of *Born To Run*), he was legally prohibited from recording until his legal problems were resolved (Sawyer 2004:9). When he finally reentered the recording studio, slightly more jaded and disillusioned with the record business after this legal struggle, it was with a stylistically more somber and adult set of songs. "After *Born To Run* I wanted to write about life in the close confines of the small towns I grew up in. . . . I felt a sense of accountability to the people I'd grown up alongside of. . . . I wanted to ensure that my music continued to have value and a sense of place" (Springsteen 2003:66). This is, after all, the desire of all great teachers—whether Buddha, Krishna, or Christ—to have their teachings remembered, valued, and heeded.

"I Believe in the Faith That Could Save Me" ("Badlands")

The strength of Springsteen's character and its reflection in his lyrics become important when critically looking at his fan following. His "value and a sense of place" are evidenced in both his writings and in his presented persona and help create a loyal and devoted fan-base. Put quite simply, fans believe what he sings and what he says. He is not seen as flawless or impervious to human failings—the breakup of his first marriage to Julianne Phillips was acted out on the pages of tabloids all over the world. Somehow, though, even this marital dissolution seemed to work in Springsteen's favor, earning him more emotional capital with his audience; he left his super-model wife for a backup singer in his band, a real "Jersey girl," Patty Scialfa, and married her. They have remained married and have three children together.

Over the course of the past 35 years, the musicians performing behind Springsteen as the E Street Band have maintained a constant lineup, with only one break from performing together. Many of these band members had played together since their teens, some members for as long as 20 years, when Springsteen released them from his employment in 1989. For reasons only truly known to Springsteen, he formed a new touring band and recorded albums without the E Streeters. Many loyal fans took this breakup hard, and never really embraced what came to be known as the "other band." For nearly 15 years the E Street Band members had been the foils for Springsteen's onstage antics, and their personas seemed entwined with Bruce's. Even the name of the band—"E Street"— harkened back to their teenage years—the house where they practiced was on E Street. Fans felt betrayed. These were extended family members, almost as much-loved as Bruce himself. (Some never truly forgave Bruce for this, and posts still regularly show up on the Internet debating the quality of the music produced with "the other band.") The E Street Band members themselves were, for the most part, silent. The "breakup" continued until January 1995, when the E Street band reunited with Bruce to record several cuts for his *Greatest Hits* compact disc. And in 1999, Springsteen accompanied by the reunited E Street Band launched their Reunion Tour, playing 120 shows in 82 countries, concluding with ten shows at New York's Madison Square Garden.

A musicologist's analysis of Springsteen's music and performance cites expression rather than "virtuosic control" as the lynchpin of his work: the audience experiences and internalizes his performance as an "honest man giving his emotional all" (Berger and Del Negro 2004:58, 59). This succinct summation says what millions of fans have been saying for over 30 years. Harris Berger and Giovanna Del Negro describe Springsteen fans as "engaging in romantic detail vertigo" and state that the listeners' attention is drawn more to the emotion and meaning than to the technical rendering of the performance (2004:59). Ultimately, these scholars maintain that this reflexivity is important to performance. Although they use the feminine pronoun, their analysis applies to males—especially Springsteen—as well:

> The reflexive metacommentary by which a performer signals her awareness of herself as a participant in an interaction—and by which she signals her awareness of the audience's attention to her—colors and informs all of the "primary" communication in the performance and plays a crucial role in the overall aesthetics of the event. (Berger and Del Negro 2004:95)

The translation of this for Springsteen and fans is that Bruce knows—as do the fans—that the audience is an integral part of the event. He in essence feeds off the crowd and gives them responsibility for a more highly charged performance or a less energetic show, playing them like another instrument in his performing repertoire, working in *concert* with the audience. For example, during a 1980 performance in Stockholm, Bruce acknowledged his growing awareness of the necessity of audience involvement:

> There's a Marvin Gaye and Tammy Terrell song: it's called "It Takes Two." In the song, Marvin Gaye sings, "It takes two to make a dream come true." And I guess that's why we're here tonight talking to you and you guys are talking to us. Because it's funny, you know, on this tour since we've been over here, I've learned . . . I've learned a lot over here. I've learned the importance of the audience, the importance of you in the show. Because we come out and we play, and we play hard and try to tell you about the things that mean a lot to us, and when you respond the way you have tonight and last night, it's like . . . it's a big, like *"me too,"* you know. It's in a buncha little things. I want you to know that it means a lot to us. (in Marsh 2004:282)

For performances during his younger years, an important part of his compact with his followers was throwing himself—literally—into the audience, being carried by their hands, and getting deposited back onto the stage with the audience's help. Today, an older Bruce, no longer anymore able to perform these strenuous physical gyrations than most of us his age, has replaced these audience-dives with moving to the edge of the stage and encouraging the lucky faithful to strum his guitar, while others touch the edges of his jeans or boots. (This held true until October 2010, when Bruce reintroduced crowd surfing during "Hungry Heart," defying his age.) As a communion of sorts, sharing guitar strings and denim instead of bread and wine, there is no fear here; Bruce trusts his audience in the same way they trust him. This is part of the covenant that has given birth to the community and the unity that fans feel with each other and with Bruce Springsteen, and that creates a climate conducive to actively paying homage to Bruce as well as to ourselves through charitable works and personal integrity:

> That's what I try to accomplish at night in a show. Presenting ideas, asking questions, trying to bring people closer to characters in the songs, closer to themselves so that they take those ideas, those questions—fundamental moral questions about the way we live and the way we behave toward one another—and then move those questions from the aesthetic into the practical, into some sort of action, whether it's action in the community, or action in the way you treat your wife, or your kid, or speak to the guy who works with you. That is what can be done, and is done, through film and music and photography and painting. Those are real changes I think you can make in people's lives. (Percy 2007)

Other spiritual traditions have expressed this in different ways. The Web site religioustolerance.org uses the term *ethics of reciprocity* to refer to the tenet that every human being has certain inherent human rights. The following are some examples, posted on religioustolerance.org, of the Golden Rule—the basic ethic of reciprocity—as found in other traditions:

> Brahmanism—"This is the sum of Dharma [duty]: Do naught unto others which would cause you pain if done to you" (Mahabharata, 5:1517).

> Buddhism—"Hurt not others in ways that you yourself would find hurtful" (Udana-Varga 5:18).

> Hinduism—"This is the sum of duty: do not do to others what would cause pain if done to you" (Mahabharata 5:1517).

> Islam—"None of you [truly] believes until he wishes for his brother what he wishes for himself" (Number 13 of Imam "Al-Nawawi's Forty Hadiths").

> Judaism—"What is hateful to you, do not to your fellow man. This is the law: all the rest is commentary" (Talmud, Shabbat 31a).

And in the Church of Bruce, do unto others becomes "Well baby you be true to me / And I'll be true to you" ("Be True"). To be "true" (to him), we need to be "true" to each other and ourselves. This message, to honor ourselves and others by acknowledging the humanity we all share, runs clear throughout his music, and his life.

Chapter 4

"Tramps Like Us"

**[Any] given cultural element is directly proportional
to the degree to which that element is reflective
of audience beliefs and values.**
(William Romanowski)

*S*pringsteen's audiences or fans, "the "faithful," in the best of moments see themselves as a reflection of the ideals espoused by Springsteen. The lyrical content of his music contained within the popular culture rubric finds itself dealing with emotions and experiences readily experienced by the majority. And because music can work as a conveyance system of shared meanings—a component of religion and culture both—the lines can further blur when sitting in the audience. George Barna's categorization of Christians suggests that those people he calls *cultural Christians* (in Romanowski 2001:28) hold this idea of works-based faith, again echoed in the Springsteen fan community. This is not to say that all Springsteen fans are either religious or Christian, however. Romanowski claims also that it is a *perspective* that makes a work religious, that "there is something right about the way he (Springsteen) creates popular music," and that the music "captures a sense of religious longing and daily struggle that resonates [with fans]" (2001:93, 30).

But what, exactly, is a *fan*? One working definition in use now, that of an enthusiastic supporter of a sports team or celebrity, differs considerably from the original definition of religious zealot (Cavicchi 1998:38). Yet, there is a component of the zealot that resides in any true fan regardless of the object of his or her passion. To be a fan indicates a certain level of devotion to the object of one's fandom. Most Springsteen fans initially become "converts" and experience this transformation through an introduction to and identification with the music and lyrics. The language these converts use is that of spiritual conversion, not unlike the language and imagery recently "saved" Christians might use, calling themselves "believers" (Steven). (My mentor and friend called this behavior "efangelism," a most apropos term.) One French fan told me that she attended her first concert in 1992 and "saw the face of God (janiss)." Some commonly used terms to describe a Springsteen event are "redemption" and "salvation," most decidedly religious, as is the burning need the converted masses feel to bring others into the fold, to convert them. Being a Springsteen fan is not unlike being a missionary for Springsteen, spreading the good word.

In the Springsteen world, there are "casual fans" and "real fans": casual fans might attend a concert but probably would not alter life-plans to do so, while real fans do whatever it takes within—and sometimes beyond—their means to attend a show. While Springsteen nation is all inclusive, the audiences are for the most part white and at least appear financially solvent. Springsteen espouses the values and trials of working-class people, but contemporary Springsteen fans are more affluent than working class, more white collar than blue. This apparently interferes not a whit with the ability of these apparently well-situated fans to embrace and extol the blue-collar virtues of hard work and hope that are entwined throughout Springsteen's songs.

Every "real" fan knows exactly how many times they have seen Springsteen, with some fans counting triple-digit performances as proof of their devotion. Springsteen fans also proclaim their solidarity with each other, casual or true, and exhibit this unity at shows by responding at various times during the performance with specific hand gestures and vocal responses. As one "follower" stated, "any one Bruce-fan could somehow speak for *all* Bruce fans . . ." part of being a Bruce fan was being a member of the shared history of the Bruce Fan Community. You knew any Bruce fan was a friend of any other Bruce fan.

> There was something about developing an audience slowly—you'd draw an audience that stood with you over a long period of time, and it got involved with the questions you were asking and the issues you were bringing up. It's an audience who you shared a history with. I saw the work that I was doing as my life's work. I thought I'd be playing music my whole life and writing my whole life, and I wanted to be a part of my audience's ongoing life. The way you do that is the same way your audience lives its life—you do it by attempting to answer the questions that both you and they have asked, sometimes with new questions. You find where those questions lead you to—your actions in the world. You take it out of the aesthetic and you hopefully bring it into your practical, everyday life, the moral or ethical. (in Percy 2007)

Who are these fans? Most are men, more evident in the European audiences than in the United States. A cursory examination of the audience in Cologne, Germany, at a December 2007 concert revealed a ballpark ratio of men to women around six to one; the Paris audience appeared even more male, with what looked to be about a ten to one ratio, male to female. Concert goers assured me that part of this was due to the "crazy Italian men fans" that traveled all over Europe following Bruce in concert. Indeed, at the Paris show of December 2007, there did look to be about 20–30 Italian men in the "Pit" (the standing area closest to the stage, reserved for general admission lottery winners) all wearing orange shirts and waving Italian flags.

A recently published book of fan stories, *For You* (Kirsch 2007), contains the fan-written and contributed stories of what Bruce means to them as well as stories relating personal encounters with him. The stories presented in the following chapters echo the same themes found in Kirsch's book, of "finding" Springsteen and what that means to the individual. These fans self-identify to whatever extent they are comfortable, using either their actual given names or screen names. In examining Kirsch's book, I tallied up the gender of the contributors and found that some 163 were identifiable as males, while 67 were women; 16 I classified as gender unknown, as the names were either unisex or unknown to me (Kirsch 2007). This supports what I have observed at concerts and the larger number of male attendees, and I will explore the possible reasons later in this chapter.

Attendance at the second *Glory Days Bruce Springsteen Symposium* also upheld my supposition about the male majority of the Church of Bruce. A cursory tally of presenters and moderators of breakout sessions from the symposium showed that the overwhelming majority were male, around 85, while only 32 women were on the schedule. Although this does not take into account those participants who may have given more than one presentation or the sessions that may have been cancelled, the numbers still support the idea that most fans are male.

In terms of age, fans run the spectrum from very young to over 60. The majority of fans seem to fall into the 40–50-year-old range. In 2007 I asked people (on a fan site where I am a member) to e-mail me and tell me a little about their "bruce-ness." Thirty-four people responded, and the majority were between the ages of 41 and 50 (thirteen). Nine people were between the ages of 31 and 40, while seven people were age 18 to 30. There were two respondents over 60, and three between 51 and 60.

For the most part, the people who communicated with me were well educated. Twelve were women, with—again—the majority being male. All but two of these particular fans had at least some college education, with two indicating a doctorate. Incomes were split almost equally for those who answered, with 17 people making less than $50,000 a year, and 17 people making more than $50,000 a year. Their occupations spanned from judges (one) and lawyers (two) to one full-time homemaker and a chef. No one reported being a manual laborer, and everyone for the most part seemed to have white-collar jobs.

This serendipitous sampling also revealed that 20 of these fans did not regularly attend any church, temple, or mosque other than the Church of Bruce; one devoted congregant however, who has attended over 14 shows and who has been a fan for 25 years, reported he was a bible student at a Jehovah Witnesses' Kingdom Hall. When asked, the fans expressed seeing no conflict between the spiritual nourishment they received through Springsteen and his music and whatever "regular" church they attended—including the Jehovah's Witness. The feeling seemed to be that whatever faith you found that helped you get through the day was valid, regardless of where you found it; finding it in Bruce just makes sense to his fans. One follower from England, a young Muslim man, did find his passion for Springsteen clashing with his ability to lead what he saw as a devout Muslim life, and he recently sold all his recordings and bootleg concerts, vowing to devote himself to his religious practice. In a private message to me, he stated that Bruce's music would be a distraction, and while it was an extremely hard choice, it was one he felt he needed to make.

One of the things I queried the cyber site about was how many times people had seen Springsteen. Answers varied from once to over 200 times, with a riotous variation between the two. I also asked about collecting concert recordings. Almost everyone collects "boots"—bootleg recordings made surreptitiously of Bruce's live performances that stretch back to the late sixties. These recordings serve as a sort of communal offering, freely traded and supplied to the faithful, all done gratuitously. Indeed, those individuals who are found to be selling these recordings and videos are severely chastised and frequently excommunicated from the loyal Springsteen congregation. At the very least, the offender's name is spread far and wide among the community, with his or her sins revealed to all via the electronic sources available to the fans—Web sites, cyber bulletin boards, and e-mails. Some of the cyber sites will ban violators and prevent their rejoining the site. Often, offenders will be inundated with nasty e-mails and private messages. This is the Springsteen community's way of maintaining social order and enforcing a social norm, a cyber take on the practice of shunning sometimes found in more orthodox religious communities such as the Mennonites and the Amish. Essentially, this creates a cyber social exile, isolated until he or she falls in line with appropriate behavior. Those who are techno-savvy can find a way around this and register at fan sites with different names, but eventually the alias usually suffers the same fate for repeated offenses. Members of these sites can also choose to "ignore" offensive posters by blocking their posts.

This (mostly) unspoken ethical rule also applies to the reselling of tickets to concerts. Springsteen tickets are among the hardest concert tickets to come by, and because of this, fans who do manage to get tickets often will get more than they personally need. These "spare" tickets are then offered up at face value or less to other fans. It is also not uncommon for fans to "faerie" (as these bestowers of spare tickets are called) others—to give away a ticket to a loyal disciple. I have been both recipient and faerie, receiving a coveted Christmas performance ticket from someone I never met, gratis, and likewise buying a ticket for someone, freely giving this to him. We have still never met but have a friendship based on our e-connection. While it may be better to give than receive, receiving is definitely a joy not to be denied! I was sent a ticket for an Atlanta performance scheduled in late April 2009, by someone I know only by screen name, with the understanding that I could pay him when I saw him; I had no hotel name, no meeting place, not even a real name for this person. I never managed to find him in Atlanta, but yes, I did send payment.

The community truly does operate on the principle of treating others as you would be treated. "The thinking is, if you're a fan of Bruce, it means you can be trusted. You're an honest person and you can sleep on my couch" (Perusse 2007). The community works on this ethical principle, again assumed to be derived from Springsteen's own actions. It's not quite WWBD (what would Bruce do), but it is close to that. Fans who act outside of the accepted behavioral parameters and violate these "bruce-ethics" (my term, not commonly used by fans) are chastised for not being "real" fans or not "listening" to Bruce; "real" fans act in accordance with the principles that they find in Springsteen's music.

"Everybody's Got a Hungry Heart" ("Hungry Heart")

"When I see Bruce Springsteen reaching to his audience—to every corner of a large arena, to every mind in the hall—I find the kind of fulfillment and community that only the best friendships and kinships might bring one, which is to say, I see an oath of love and meaning played out with a full heart" (Mikal Gilmore in Marsh 2004:433–34).

While I have personally only attended concerts in three different countries—France, Germany, and the United States—I have nevertheless met fans from at least 11 different countries, and not always in the context of a concert. The connection is the same with these fans as with my own compatriots—all things Bruce ties us together. Courtesies are extended and trust freely given, simply on the basis of our mutual efangelism and membership in the Church of Bruce. My first experience meeting a foreign Bruce-fan happened in 2004, in Northern Ireland. Through a mutual friend, also someone whom I had never met, I was given the name and phone number of a family living outside Belfast—Mom and Dad were both avid fans and members of a cyber bulletin board sponsored by Sony Music—brucespringsteen.net. In spite of our all being members of this site, I had never "spoken" to or communicated at all with J. or D. until we actually arrived in Northern Ireland. I called, introduced myself and told them my screen name, and we made plans to meet that week. My traveling companion and partner in crime and I arrived early one afternoon at their lovely cottage and immediately jumped head-first into Bruce-lore, comparing concerts and favorite songs. As is often the case, the in-country fans became local tour guides, taking us to a number of nearby attractions. We had a wonderful time, and when we left we were no longer strangers. To this day, I still get a holiday card from them.

During a recent trip to Europe to observe Springsteen and fans, I met a number of other concert goers from all over Europe, as well as some expatriate Americans. The language and emotions expressed by the Europeans echoed that of American fans, even if the audience responses differed slightly. Euro fans tend to be more enthusiastic and loud, waving and clapping in a hypnotic, synchronized motion. One German fan in front of me in line said that every man wants to *be* him while every woman wants to *meet* him. Another Danish fan who had driven eight hours to see a show in Berlin, and who had just finished driving another five to get to Cologne, said he traveled to see Bruce as much as he could. I also was assured that the German audience at this show would make American audiences pale in comparison, a point of great pride for the Europeans. Hobbs, a German fan, proudly showed me a tattoo of Bruce's signature right where he'd signed her arm. She expressed the idea that Bruce was her emotional and spiritual light in a dark reality.

Aussiebrucefan is a drug and alcohol rehabilitation counselor who says he was attracted to Bruce because of the "music, lyrics, and social responsibility thing." S, also from Australia, says she can't wait to make the Asbury pilgrimage during the next tour. Springsteen has appeared in Australia and New Zealand, but not with any sort of regularity, and so fans "down under" must travel to him. Corvettesue, from New Zealand, says that "integrity and Bruce" have given her a whole new life and many friends where she once had few. In talking, she also used the term "Church of Bruce," and when I commented that he didn't give us actual direction, she vehemently replied, "But he does." These fans see the guidance and moral challenges set forth in

Springsteen's music as guidelines and suggestions for a mode of behavior in their personal lives, much as a member of any religious community follows the examples set by its spiritual leader. It is not necessary for Springsteen to say "This is what you must do or not do." His songs, if looked at as parables, contain their own moral, their own cause-and-effect outcome. Blueguitar, an American, had this to say:

> He was great, but flawed as we all are. He knew it, and wasn't afraid to admit it. A rock and roller? Sure, but to me he was so much more. He inspired me to do more with my life, to go out into the world and make a difference. To do *my* job a little better, just like he did. To know you had given your all, just like he did. I believe in the power and faith that Bruce Springsteen preaches about.

Fan all4eddie took his autistic son to a recent concert, along with a particularly meaningful sign he wanted Bruce to read:

> Bruce stopped playing, read every word, and seemed to be a little choked up . . . then he reaches out and hands Eddie his harmonica, needless to say the tears began to flow, my hands were shaking as they are now retelling this story . . . our sign read "Your music taught our autistic son to speak."

Brianzai says Bruce provides "a place of mercy and healing." Hanaree says "it again feels like God speaking directly to me through these words: 'I will provide for you / I'll stand by your side / you'll need a good companion for this part of the ride' . . . Bruce provides spiritual connection." BjorntorunMN says that Bruce was the one thing that provided him comfort on "those dark nights" after a bad divorce and job loss. And Rev. S. Meyer says: "Bruce incarnates his message, becomes a conduit for hope" and calls his concerts "nothing less than revival meetings" (personal communication 1/21/08).

Clearly for these fans, Springsteen provides spiritual sustenance and all that implies: hope, understanding, forgiveness, despair, joy, and redemption, as well as community and acceptance and a connection to something ineffable and greater than the sum of all these parts. There is a spiritual element here that works as well as any religious service. One of the common threads that run through most fan meet-ups is the initial "witnessing" that takes place; each person wants to relate his or her conversion story, to share how he or she "came" to Bruce. The discussions usually then migrate to "what's your favorite song?" and "how many times have you seen him?" In an odd sort of way, these add social capital to the exchange—the more shows, the greater number of "Bruce-points." (Show veterans occupy a place of respect and authority, and are seen by some as more knowledgeable of the lore.) This also serves as a way of making an initial connection to each other, and in some fashion, validating one's character. To generalize, the more avid a fan, the greater the internalization of the message conveyed through the performance, and therefore, the more trustworthy the person. This social mechanism is not unlike Navajo clans that define to whom you are related and from whom you can seek assistance.

When discussing any given show, fans will not only ask how the band sounded but also what Bruce's energy was like, as well as how the audience responded. Missed cues or sour notes play less into the fans' enjoyment than the experience as a whole. Flaws in the performance sometimes actually seem to enhance the experience, personalizing it. Seeing the human side of Springsteen and the band in the form of forgotten lyrics or missed cues comes to be endearing and relished as a shared human experience between fan and performer. (There is at present at least one online discussion over the "worst" song performance in Bruce's concert history.) The feeling that Bruce is human, and subject to human foibles like the rest of us, comforts us, as does the idea that "we" are an important component of the performance. In essence, his flawed performance underscores his humanity, illustrating that even the best among us is flawed by definition of being human.

"Meet Me at Mary's Place, We're Gonna Have a Party" ("Mary's Place")

Outside of the performances, fans commune online at one of several cyber fan sites discussing a myriad of topics, not all limited to Springsteen-world. Membership on these sites is free and most are open to anyone with the exception of several sites that are by invitation only; memberships on the open sites number in the thousands. At www.greasylake.org, membership stands at 13,131, while www.backstreets.com boasts over 44,000. These cyber communities offer a way to connect with like-minded people and talk. There are forums for discussing just-Bruce-related topics and activities, forums for musicians seeking and finding song chords, forums for acquiring copies of compact disks of entire concerts that have been surreptitiously recorded, listings of YouTube videos and available MP3s, and others for just general discussion and moral support. It is on these Web sites that the feeling of community becomes accentuated and nurtured. There are parties planned, softball games organized, and personal alliances set up. Sometimes there is also a charitable component to these gatherings, with money donated to a specific cause—Second Harvest Food Bank, The Danny Federici Melanoma Fund, and so forth. The gatherings I have attended have been as small as 11 members and as large as nearly 100. (The summer tailgates rank among my best gathering memories, as the food was always spectacular.) One Web site routinely gathers to collect and mail care packages to U.S. troops stationed overseas. This site also organizes get-togethers not planned around concerts—events like wine-tasting parties and ski trips to Vermont—for its members. This particular fan site has a large number of fans who have become fast friends in real life, and they interact on a fairly regular basis even when Springsteen is not touring.

When a tour is in full swing, fans "gather" at their computers and on their chosen Web site during the showtime of whatever city Springsteen and company are performing in. Fans chat and await word of what is being performed, vicariously experiencing the show. Called the "set-list watch," a fan at the concert text messages or calls someone else to post on the Internet what is being played so that the "watchers" can keep track of the songs played. This functions as a kind of roundtable, where small talk is exchanged and personal experiences shared while waiting the three to six minutes it takes for the present song to be completed. During the most recent tour in 2009 (as of this writing), a new cyber gadget allowed a fan to stream the concerts live if someone called her from inside the venue. Fans also keep track of where those Web site members inside the venue are in relation to the stage, a kind of vicarious experience. While nowhere close to the experience of being at the show, the set-list watch helps to expand each cyber participant's knowledge of and relation to the other fans online participating. After the show, attendees will post their impressions and reviews for those who were not there, all of which serves to reinforce the inclusiveness and community on the "boards" and in the greater Springsteen community.

I attempted, with only one success, to get a webmaster from these various Web fan sites to speak with me about that person's involvement with the Springsteen community and his or her personal objective when founding a site, but only one of the site administrators responded to me. And the nature of the World Wide Web and cyber technology problems—site crashes and data loss—prevents me from delving into the archives of these sites to retrieve their history. I do know the history of the ThunderRoad Web site (http://S15.invisionfree.com/ThunderRoad), a small, intimate invitation-only fan site that was created by a Canadian fan when a number of members from a different Web site decided they would form a site with their own rules of conduct. The site is well moderated, and political discussion is not allowed. Membership is 198 fans, but total posts number over 678,000. From the Web site: "Our intent is to keep the membership open but to those who truly want to be part of this community for what it is . . . a place to get away and hang comfortably with respect for members and non-members alike. Like all boards, we know it won't be everyone's cup of tea." The moderators on any given Web site monitor postings for language and demeanor, and any post found to violate the Web site's rules is deleted, with possible sanctions meted out to the offender. Some of ThunderRoad's lengthy behavior guidelines to new members include:

> Posts that contain the following are NOT permitted:
> - those with profane, threatening, abusive, racist or otherwise offensive language
> - those with an excessive use of foul language
> - those that threaten another member or non-member's privacy
> - those that contain offensively explicit sexual content
>
> If you have any questions, please feel free to PM a Moderator or e-mail us at: mods.thunderroad@gmail.com

The Web site www.backstreets.com posted the following terms that must be agreed to before a party may register to use the site:

> You agree not to post any abusive, obscene, vulgar, slanderous, hateful, threatening, sexually-orientated or any other material that may violate any laws be it of your country, the country where "BTX" is hosted or International Law. Doing so may lead to you being immediately and permanently banned, with notification of your Internet Service Provider if deemed required by us. The IP address of all posts are recorded to aid in enforcing these conditions. You agree that "BTX" have the right to remove, edit, move or close any topic at any time should we see fit. As a user you agree to any information you have entered to being stored in a database. While this information will not be disclosed to any third party without your consent, neither "BTX" nor php BB shall be held responsible for any hacking attempt that may lead to the data being compromised.

Backstreets.com has a home page that offers a variety of functions, from recent news articles to links for set-lists, available music downloads, the Backstreets shop that sells all manner of Bruce-related items, and BTX, the backstreets ticket exchange. BTX offers members seven different forums for posting and conversing on a variety of subjects: the promised land forum is reserved for conversations strictly about Springsteen and company; the ticket-sellers as well as ticket-needers forums are venues to obtain or sell tickets to various concerts, and not solely for Springsteen shows; the vineyard is a music-sharing forum, while the political world is the place for discussing world events and politics, and the loose-ends forum is for non-Springsteen chatter. Both alliances and enemies can be made on any of these forums. Presently, the political world forum has been closed due to unruly online behavior and violations of the site rules that members agreed to when they joined. BTX, as members know it, has a large and ever-growing membership, and a reputation among online Springsteen fans as a home to some contentious and unpleasant posters. The online community tries to maintain order among their own, but being so large, some nastiness slips by. Currently, total posts hover around 933,000.

Stone Pony London (SPL) (www.stoneponylondon.net) is a European-hosted site, again serving multiple purposes, from disseminating news to organizing group trips to see Springsteen. In the online Springsteen community, SPL has a reputation as being a Web site for the hard-core fan, those seized by the need to know all there is to know about all facets of Springsteen, from song analysis to the best sounding bootlegs and beyond. At present, membership is 3,521 with a post count in the vicinity of 313,000; there are 16 forums on which to post.

Greasylake.org is administered from Denmark and, as with the other Web sites mentioned, has a number of different forums for members' use. The site is well moderated, and posting behavior is closely monitored by the various "mods" (moderators). This was the first Web site I discovered when I began my journey with Bruce, and it has been a valuable resource for my concert-going experiences, my bootleg collecting (a member here supplied me with my very first bootleg), and my research. The very first Bruce-fans I connected with were members of this Web site, and in no small fashion responsible for my growing interest in the fan congregation. The Web site offers this description:

> Greasy Lake is a fan-based, fan-operated Bruce Springsteen Web site. That means we have no relations and no contact to Bruce Springsteen or his management whatsoever. We do this in our spare time and we do it for free for the benefit of all the like-minded people out there. The goal is to make Greasy Lake informative, entertaining, and a rally point to Bruce-fans everywhere.

The webmaster from greasylake.org (GL, as we "locals" call it) responded to my inquiry about the site's history; he and a friend started a site called Open All Night in 1996. In 1998, the name changed to Greasy Lake and had around 20 visitors a day. The site began to grow with the reunion of Springsteen and the E Street Band in 1999–2000, and a core of "regulars" developed. CosmicKid, the founder of greasylake.org, explains what the site means to him, in spite of the enormous amount of work involved:

> It wasn't till *The Rising* Tour that the site grew to what we know today with thousands of members and upward 100 people online at a time on a normal day during prime time. It's really been an amazing ride. The site has gone through ups and downs. We've had our share of conflicts, but it's always been overshadowed by the amazing sense of community and how people have made it part of their real lives by meeting up with other members, forming friendships, and even couples. The first GL wedding was in 2001 when thundrrds and Ace were married. There was even a

collection among the members to get me over there to the wedding. A collection organized by Glory Roads, who, incidentally, is now my wife. So for me personally and a lot of members, GL has come to mean an awful lot. (CosmicKid)

There are any number of other "boards" for Springsteen fans, but to my knowledge, these are the sites with the highest profiles, and the ones that I frequent. As the posted rules indicate, these fan communities have social norms and standards as with any community in real life (IRL—as the cyber community says). Likewise, some posters hold a more "esteemed" position in their community, having built their credibility over years of posting. Each board has its own particular flavor; many fans cross-post and are members of several boards/communities. For me, each serves a different function. When I want a lighthearted exchange, I go to one board; for information, I go to another. One site has the best links to available downloads, while another has a more intellectual level of conversation, and I am constantly enlightened about some event or other. But the overriding, uniting element is Bruce Springsteen. If we are a congregation, the boards could be seen as sects, offering a different facet of Springsteen-life. Perhaps a more useful metaphor would be to see the congregation as Protestant, and the message boards as representing different denominations of Protestantism: while we all "believe" in the same thing, we exhibit our belief in slightly different ways. And as any congregation shares its triumphs and defeats, these boards function in the same way: posters share their sorrows and losses, announce births, weddings, graduations and military postings; seek prayers for the ill; and generally help lessen the burdens of a solitary heart.

These boards, for the most part, are composed of caring individuals who are ready to lend an ear or a helping hand. But as happens in real life and because everyone has a different personality, sometimes it becomes necessary for the online community to police itself. Inappropriate behavior and language is usually addressed by a board moderator, if one exists, who metes out suspensions and sanctions for those individuals violating a standard. As mentioned earlier, offenses can include selling bootleg recordings or tickets at inflated prices. But there are other less obvious offenses that often result in sanctions. Some boards will ask for foul language to be tempered, while other sites prohibit sexist or racist language. Sanctions can range from a suspension of posting privileges to permanent banning and revocation of posting privileges. And as happens in the real world, sometimes the board denizens are subject to fraud.

Early in 2010, a post was made on backstreets.com alerting members to the death of a fairly high-profile member. This man had been generous over the years, graciously sharing his trove of bootlegs with other members, and sharing stories of his life's trials and tribulations with the community. When his friend came on the board and posted news of his death, many members were shocked and saddened. The outpouring of sympathy and goodwill was immediate and intense, and members began to organize a memorial. Plans were made to attend baseball games in his memory (his screen name was Mrbaseball907) and to distribute baseball caps displaying his screen name. People from all over the world came together to try and make these things happen, sending checks and offering emotional support. Every Sunday, Tom Cunningham hosts a show entitled "Bruce Brunch" from 9:00 AM until 11:00 AM on radio station 105.7 The Hawk; January 31 was dedicated to this "deceased" fan (backstreets.com/btx/viewtopic.php?f=2&t=196462). However, shortly after this, it came to light that MrBaseball907 was in fact *not* dead, and board members quickly turned on him as well as some of the people involved with the various tribute initiatives. The episode became even more bizarre, as details began to trickle in about this supposedly dead man and his life's trials. An article on tampabay.com tells the bizarre story of this man who faked his own death, even to the point of a published obituary (Krause 2010). Since this odd event in January, members of the Springsteen backstreets community have largely expunged this man from the online community and mended relations with each other. It is doubtful that MrBaseball907's indiscretions will ever be forgotten or forgiven, and the community at backstreets.com is today perhaps more cynical and suspicious because of him. Members' reactions varied, but as rosie3030 said:

> The headline was wrong, it didn't tear us apart. We are OK, we're still here. There was arguing and there were hurt feelings for sure, but the real story is that it was done *to* us, not the understandable conflicts we had when it started to become known what had happened. People who read this, who don't know us, may think we're naive but we know "us" better. Long live BTX! (www.backstreets.com/btx/viewtopic.php?f=2&t= 198391&start=15 [2/26/10])

Making Grown Men Cry

Having seen Bruce Springsteen and the E Street Band only once while under the age of 50, December 3, 1975, I remember that the people in the audience mostly looked more like me than not. In contrast, the audience at my second show, November 21, 1999, was mainly middle-aged and male. In fact, it was the behavior of the men in the audience that initially caught my eye, as I have rarely seen men as demonstrative and emotional in a public setting that was not a baseball game. This was different from the emotion and ardor of male fans at sporting events. Sporting events become rowdy and loud, but the participation is more that of spectator than participant. Men yell and show spontaneous eruptions of enthusiasm, but there is a detachment, a space between the fan and the game. The fan observes and responds to the action in the game on different levels: his team has scored; a favorite player has made an exceptional play—either good or bad; the opposing team has scored/missed a play. The fan reactions can be either positive and celebratory, or negative and mournful, and there will be both kinds simultaneously in any given venue, since team sports require two teams.

A Springsteen concert audience more closely resembles a church congregation. There are no teams involved, and so, to stay with the sports metaphor, the audience members are all on the same side, cheering for the same team. The men participate wholeheartedly, singing and dancing and pumping their fists. One man, a self-described simple Cajun boy pseudo-intellectual from the bayous of Louisiana turned Manhattanite, describing his first concert, said it "reminded me of things I'd seen and heard about taking place in Pentecostal tent revivals in the South. Grown men crying, people running up and down dancing in the aisles, people dropping to their knees in quasi deity worship, et cetera" (cajunboyinthecity).

Springsteen is not unaware himself of the sexual makeup of his fans. In an interview with *60 Minutes'* Scott Pelley on July 27, 2008, when asked why he still toured, Bruce responded by asking what other job he could have that would make "grown men cry and women dance." In the past, he has also made mention of seeing bald heads in the audience and jokingly expressed concern that the faces he sees closest to the stage are men's faces. At the 2004 Rock and Roll Hall of Fame Induction Ceremony for Jackson Browne, Bruce said: "While the E Street Band and I were sweating our asses off to draw rooms filled with men, Jackson was drawing more women than an Indigo Girls show" (www.spinner.aol.com/rockhall). Indeed, the Pit area (the area on the floor of concert venues that is reserved for general admission lottery winners) at any given Springsteen show will inevitably be filled with a majority of males.

Many men bring their sons, and the concert becomes a bonding ceremony of sorts for them—or at least for the fathers. Many of the 30-something male fans I met reported that they were taken to their first Springsteen show by their fathers, and hence dad gets the credit for their conversions. At any given concert one can see young men with their fathers, and fathers with young children beside them. At the Giants Stadium Springsteen show in October 2009, I met a three-generational family of men attending the show together. Grandfather had introduced father to Springsteen's music when father was in his mid-teens, and now father was introducing his son, only nine but eager, to the music and the congregation. They declined to be named here, but assured me that the nine-year-old was a willing participant. At this same show, another father and son duo—dad age 40 or so and son eightish—told me that this was in fact the son's fourth show and that the young man knew the words to all the songs in Springsteen's prodigious repertoire. They were both indeed singing along to every number that night.

At summer concerts and tailgates an observer would immediately notice the clusters of men barbecuing and blasting Springsteen on their car stereos. I have stopped and spoken with many of these men, and a fair amount of them are longtime childhood fans who have been coming together to see Bruce for years. In the parking lot of the Sheraton Meadowlands, I shared a drink and a song with six young men, age 25–35 (I failed to ask their exact ages), a combination of cousins and longtime friends who never missed the opportunity to see Bruce together. Bruce's maleness, combined with a safe place—a sacred space?—to be vulnerable allows these men to feel the emotional bond between them in a way they can accept and deal with.

In November 2009 I attended what will come to be known as a legendary show at New York City's Madison Square Garden. A young man, Carl, in his early 30s, had traveled from Germany for this show and the next without tickets (we secured them successfully). He told me his big dream was to be able to bring his stepson, who was only two and afflicted with Muscular Dystrophy, along with his baby daughter to some future show, sharing his love of Bruce with them. His stepson, he says, "moves his small legs well when Max plays the drums." Carl's experience with his own father was slightly different, as he introduced his father to the music, and not the reverse. In a poignant message, Carl said:

> Early 1985, when I was 15, my father once came into my room and heard me play "The River" by Bruce Springsteen. He also loved that song, and asked me if I could record it for him. I was so happy. I felt appreciated; and that we were really becoming "friends," sharing something. I had always been enjoying his music collection. I made a tape for his birthday that May. He died a couple months later in an accident. One year later, Springsteen released his *Live 75–85* set, with this long introduction into "The River" and his story about his father. I have cried many tears ever since, when I listened to that long intro. I often wondered, how my life would have been like, could I have shared more with him.

Springsteen's concert stories about his relationship with his father are legendary and indicate that he had a tumultuous and often strained connection with his dad, which may offer some insight as to why men connect with him. In an April 2, 1996, interview published in *The Advocate,* Springsteen said:

> I think when I was growing up, that was difficult for my dad to accept that I wasn't like him. I was different. Or maybe I was like him, and he

didn't like that part of himself—more likely. I was gentle and . . . a sensitive kid. . . . But basically for me, that lack of acceptance was devastating, really devastating. (Weider 2004:218)

Springsteen has addressed his "issues" with his dad over the course of his career, lyrically in song and with his stage-confessional stories in concert. (As mentioned previously, over the years Springsteen and his father reconciled.)

These stories strike a chord with many of his male fans, prompting reminiscence such as the following from anotherthinline: "'Independence Day' made me tear up as I listened to the lyrics and thought of my dad and the relationship we never got to have . . . my problems didn't go away last night, but for a few hours I got to dance all over them" (http://wordpress.com). By attempting to share a love of something intrinsically important, these fathers are attempting to prevent or close emotional gaps between themselves and their sons. "Elvis is alive," a fan from Glasgow said. He continued, "My own favourite memory is of taking my 17-year-old, know-all son, to the Hampden Park gig earlier this year. It was his first Bruce gig. He arrived a skeptic and left a fanatic. Bruce does that."

While I am not discussing fathers and daughters or mothers and daughters sharing Bruce-moments, I have anecdotally observed that the greatest emotional distances and conflicts often seem to be between parents and children who are the same sex; however, I make no clinical claims nor offer up psychological research to support this observation. That is a topic unto itself to be addressed in another venue and at another time. But to balance the scales, here is what ericm104 had to say about seeing Springsteen with his daughter:

I was there with my daughter and went through exactly the same emotions. At the end of "Backstreets" she turned to me and said, "Wow, that was something else," and there I was wiping the tears away and said, "Tell me about it." She was like, "It's OK Dad, there's a lot of people here crying right now." I'll never forget that show, the emotions of the band and crowd, the intensity of the night, and the way the crowd and band pulled each other through the show. I got teary during "Sandy" and "Racing" that night also, and a few more times during the show. Never happened to me before at a Bruce show. (www.backstreets.com)

As previously stated, the European audiences are even more visibly male than U.S. audiences. The level of emotional openness exhibited by many male Springsteen fans surprised me, as the men that I personally know are not particularly demonstrative. This openness and emotional candor may be a direct product of lyrics that espouse real feelings in a nonoverly sentimental fashion. Bruce Springsteen, who is in top physical condition, appears to be a man's man yet he is unafraid to express his inner thoughts. Jjmiller made this observation at a *Rising* Tour show in 2003:

Sure, I've teared up a few times. But in 2003 on *The Rising* Tour, we were in the PIT for a show at Giants Stadium. We noticed a guy next to us who was there by himself. He took his jacket off halfway through the show and I noticed a NYFD tattoo on his bicep. When Bruce played "Into the Fire," this guy just starts weeping. That kinda weeping was contagious. Next thing you know everyone around him was crying and patting this guy on the back. Most moving moment at any Bruce show I've ever been to. (www.backstreets.com)

Some of his finest and most poignant songs are about friendship, and on stage he is visibly affectionate with his band mates. After a solo, he will cross the stage to embrace or kiss Clarence Clemons, his saxophone player of nearly 40 years; performances themselves usually end with hugs all around for the E Street Band members. And there are tears, from time to time, such as at the final performance of *The Rising* Tour in 2003. One other exceptionally emotional show was the one performed on April 22, 2008, in Tampa, Florida, just one day after the funeral of E Street member Danny Federici. Danny and Bruce had played together since their teenage years, and his death deeply affected Springsteen. Said moe_howard2 on the backstreets.com message board:

I was at the show in Tampa the day after Danny's funeral. Man for the first 5 songs there wasn't a dry eye in the house including Bruce. I went into thinking, OK be a man you are not going to cry. Then they played "Blood Brothers" with the video tribute, that got the ball rolling. After that was over they had a spotlight on the organ that Danny would have played and no one at it and started playing "Backstreets," that pretty much took care of my machoness that I wasn't going to cry.

Fan happyface said of this same evening:

The opening of the concert was one of the most emotional musical experiences I've ever gone through. Just seeing the band walk onstage in the darkness and the opening montage start playing, the tear ducts definitely started getting filled. And then when the band kicked into "Backstreets," that performance was intensely emotional. Every howl and word he sang into the microphone was filled with the pain and the loss Bruce was experiencing, and everyone else there felt it too.

Any Springsteen fan site will have dozens—if not hundreds—of similar posts, expressing the same kind of emotional response to either a recording or a live show.

One of the more unconventional stage actions of Springsteen's career was the "soul kiss" (Lombardi 1988:12). The soul kiss occurred at the end of "Thunder Road," and was a full-fledged lip-lock between Clarence and Bruce (see www.youtube.com/watch?v=WaLsE-HufG8&feature=related). This stage act continued through much of the 1980s tours; whatever speculation there was about Bruce's intent with this kiss, fans seemed unaffected and his sexual orientation remained securely male. It may be that by acting freely in a public venue in front of thousands of fans, Bruce changed the paradigm of maleness and contributed greatly to the freeing of the psyches of his male fans. Being openly and visibly affectionate and emotional became more acceptable, allowing emotional latitude unavailable to them previously. As bosshawg said, again on the back-streets.com message board, "I cry way too much at Bruce's shows . . . but it's also the only time I ever cry . . . so it's welcomed." Many men may share this feeling, that there is a safe zone at a Springsteen concert where they can freely experience a full range of emotions without being afraid of being seen.

In a paper presented at the second *Glory Days Symposium,* Rosalie Z. Fanshel explored the ambiguity in both Bruce Springsteen's lyrics and stage performance. Calling the rock and roll world a "prime example of a homosocial landscape" (Fanshel 2009:3), she points to the areas where Springsteen's persona works in dissonance with his lyrical world. The term homosocial refers to a nonsexual same-sex relationship of a type found in the military, fraternities, sports, and yes, Springsteen concerts to a lesser degree. This perspective makes more normative the previously mentioned "soul kiss." By Bruce's blurring the line between relationships, behaviors between men have a newly expanded range of emotions available to them, and an openness toward other men not often seen outside of the institutions mentioned above. One fan, westcoast, says:

> The first time I heard him do "Thunder Road" I teared up. I couldn't figure out why I would do that and was self-conscious about it. Then I looked up and this very large fierce looking man next to me was also crying, only he didn't seem at all concerned about it. Bruce is about being real and caring about the important things.

Even younger male friends succumb to the emotions: "When Bruce started 'Backstreets' in Richmond I leaned over to my friend and said I didn't know if I was going to get through this one without crying. I'm a 17-year-old athlete ha ha, I managed to get through it, but I was sooo close" (obxsully).

Fanshel also notes that Bruce has fuzzied the black-and-white areas of sexual orientation in his lyrics and performances, expressing "deep love between men that is often explicitly romantic and sexual" (2009:3). There is a fluidity in his writing and actions that make these emotions normative, and not outside socially accepted behaviors. The Springsteen community has been debating the sex of characters in some songs for decades, with no resolution: Bobby Jean in "Bobby Jean"; Terry in "Backstreets"; the status of Frank to the narrator in "This Hard Land"; the barefoot street boys and the golden-heeled fairies in "Incident on 57th Street." Martha Nell Smith says that

Springsteen's stage performances are "permeated" with homoeroticism and that in his "artistic maneuvers" he assumes the feminine: "though he writes and sings about Adam, he finally seems much more like Eve in his approach to knowledge" (1991:849). In *Born in the USA: Bruce Springsteen and the American Tradition,* author Jim Cullen notes the "intensely social quality of his settings . . ." in Springsteen's songs, and comments on the nearly "pack mentality characteristics of young males . . ." along with the "almost erotic subtext" that drive these characters (2005:126).

Several songs have been written from the female perspective or using a female narrator, and yes, female fans acknowledge his ability to understand and empathize with the feminine viewpoint. Springsteen's message essentially then becomes gender-free and accommodates all sexual orientations without prejudice—all are welcome in the Springsteen congregation. His personal orientation never comes under question, and is neither necessary nor important, because rock and roll has the power to bring people together, and no one does that better than Bruce Springsteen and the E Street Band. When the lights go down and the band walks onstage, an "overwhelming sense of love, joy, and total rockin' commitment fills the room night after night" (sweetlight). And that is all that matters.

Chapter 5

Community in the
E Street Nation

"Now you can't break the ties that bind"
("The Ties That Bind")

*B*ecause the word "community" is so overworked and overused, lumping together any loose association from car owners to cell phone service providers, it is necessary to specify exactly how I am using it in the context of the Bruce Springsteen fan community. Social science literature provides many different conceptual ideas of what constitutes community. The term has been used in the past to identify an actual geographical location as well as to indicate a connection with others who share common customs and identities (Brown 2002:3). In his 1995 book, Amitai Etzioni described the important aspects of community: "What is needed, rather, is a strengthening of the bonds that tie people to one another, enabling them to overcome isolation and alienation . . . to establish in communities the moral voice that leads people to encourage one another to behave more virtuously than they would otherwise" (1995:iii). In this sense, the Springsteen fan community can be situated within the parameters of Etzioni's description; Bruce is that moral voice that ties us together, acting as the catalyst to help overcome this isolation and alienation.

The fan community also occupies a geographical space, but that space is fluid, changing from one concert venue to another, in this sense creating a global community. The concert audience in one country will have fans from any number of countries who have traveled to see Springsteen and to meet others who share their love of his music. I have met fans from Denmark, Italy, England, Ireland, Sweden, Norway, Germany, Canada, Singapore, Scotland, France, and Australia at concerts in New Jersey, as well as at concerts in Cologne, Germany, and Paris, France. Indeed, I have met some of these same fans in New Jersey *and* Europe. Seeing joanfontaine on the steps of the venue in Paris was comforting, and sharing a beer in Cologne with killiefrombuffalo lessened my embarrassment over my lack of language skills.

If a "community" needs a unifying principle, as some scholars have said (Keller 2003:3), the Springsteen community has that in the music, performances, and person of Springsteen. Fans are able to overcome feelings of isolation, if only temporarily and occasionally, when in the presence—real-time or cyberspace—of other fans who understand how they feel. Yet, some scholars have defined this feeling as communitarianism rather than community: "to qualify for community, social categorizations must be translated into a consciousness of a kind, a sense of belonging, and a shared identity, past or future" (Keller 2003:8). Community is then concrete and rooted in place, while communitarianism is abstract and more a set of moral principles (Keller 2003).

In the sense that our shared identity is Bruce, the Springsteen fan community somewhat fulfills the criteria for both community and communitarianism. In this day and age we need to reconfigure the idea of community and eliminate the requirement of a geographic location, because for many of us, community rooted in place no longer exists. Many of us no longer belong to a worship group or know the names of our neighbors. We must now give consideration to the cyber communities of which so many people are members. These online "communities" help to fulfill the need we all crave to fill "regardless of race, gender, culture, or social class: acceptance" (Bugeja 2005:1). While people may want to posit that the age of technology has adversely affected us and created a sense of isolation—each of us alone at our keyboards—in this Internet age the World Wide Web has become a "hometown" (Bugeja 2005:3). "Neighbors" are as close as our keyboard and our Internet connection; this may be as good as it gets for those who immerse themselves in video games and online communication, a surrogate for live, human connection (Waldinger 2005). Springsteen fans make use of these virtual-communities—"social aggregations that emerge from the [Internet] to form webs of personal relationships in cyberspace" (Rheingold 1993:5). These cyber sites are usually fan run, and offer a glimpse into the Springsteen-fan world. They represent community, organized around a unifying principle (Springsteen and his music) and fill a variety of functions. The fan site serves as a place to discuss current and personal events, share emotions, get the latest updates on the musician's activities and news, and form friendships.

Writing about the Protestant church in 1978, Wade Clark Roof describes the "primacy of belonging" aspect of community:

> Participation in the religious community exposes the believer to others sharing the faith, which, in turn, helps to reinforce personal commitments . . . religion fulfills a quasi-ethnic role in providing a sense of belonging, the meaning aspects of religion . . . intimately rooted in the belonging. (Roof 1978:54)

Following this reasoning, Bruce followers are therefore members not only of the same "church" but also of their own "ethnic" group, with a shared culture. Attending concerts reaffirms the belief in Bruce and in the fan-community solidarity, resulting in the E Street nation and the Church of Bruce.

Several of the larger Springsteen fan cyber sites are administered and moderated by non-American fans (further indicating his popularity outside the United States). CosmicKid is the Danish architect and founder of one of the largest of these fan sites, greasylake.org. He saw his first Bruce concert in 1988 and was dramatically impacted by it:

> Something had changed in me. When I realized the possibilities of the Internet I knew I'd found my medium. . . . Real people getting together over a shared passion. And real people, strangers, once again grabbing each other's hands, if only virtually, just like I'd seen them do that night . . . a life-altering experience that I still feel today. It's been one hell of a ride and still is.

CosmicKid is only one of many fervent non-American followers, and he like many of the others has made the "pilgrimage" to Asbury Park and the legendary bar, the Stone Pony, where Bruce was a regular fixture early in his career. Pilgrimage happens in many spiritual traditions, these journeys to whatever is iconic and meaningful within that belief system; sometimes it is a tree-covered hillside, sometimes it is a tomb, or a temple, and sometimes it is a signpost on a street corner. Visitors can take a tour of Asbury Park and Freehold, New Jersey, seeing the places mentioned in Springsteen's earlier songs, and the sites of his youth (www.njrockmap.com). Almost every European fan, whom I've spoken with and who has visited the United States, has made it a point to make this pilgrimage and eat pizza at Federicci's, have a beer at the Stone Pony, take their picture in front of Madame Marie's fortune-telling stand, and cruise down Kingsley—all places and things that have meaning for the fan and that are part of the Springsteen mythology. (Guided walking tours are available with advanced planning.) These pilgrimages are not unlike the Holy Land tours I observed when in Israel, with pilgrims eager to walk the same ground that Jesus, Mohammed, and Moses all walked.

In October 2009, I had the great pleasure of taking two friends from France to make their pilgrimage to Asbury Park and surroundings. I became acquainted with J by way of the Web sites we mutually posted on, and we had become friendly. J and S live in Paris and had hosted my friend and me when we were there to see Bruce in December of 2007. J had been wanting to see a show in New Jersey and finally made the decision to travel to the United States to see one of the last-ever shows to be held at Giants Stadium. And while we did not have the necessary time to do the complete tour, the complete pilgrimage, we hit the highlights, snapping photos on the Asbury Park boardwalk, in front of Madame Marie's, and in front of Convention Hall. We ventured further down the beach, south to Freehold, and posed at the corner of Tenth Avenue and E Street, where a couple from California took our pictures. "We understand," they said. My Parisian friends were excited to be visiting places once familiar to them only in song, and even photographed the exit signs on the Garden State Parkway. By doing this, making this pilgrimage, we became in some small and magic way part of the songs and active participants in the stories and legends we have heard throughout the years of our Brucedom. For foreign fans especially, this creates a common frame of reference for them and offers a window into a life they might otherwise not know, at least not as intimately.

We ended our mini-pilgrimage with the concert that brought J and S to the United States followed by an after-show wind-down at our hotel. The Sheraton had turned into Springsteen central this weekend, and the E Street Band played over the sound system throughout the hotel's lobby and hallways. (The front-desk staff told me that over three-quarters of the rooms reserved were booked because of the Springsteen shows scheduled for that Wednesday, Friday, and Saturday at Giants Stadium.) Energized and exhausted fans told endless stories over drinks to total strangers, and for a while, it felt as if no one wanted to leave the group-joy experience. We seemed to fall chronologically, the oldest of us giving in to exhaustion first; the Bruce afterburn lasts too brief a time.

I posed the question of what the fan community formed around the message boards meant to the people frequenting these sites, and the responses I received indicated the similar and repeated belief that anyone who is a fan of Bruce is welcome; likewise, the fans on these sites felt at ease, at home. "We are a group of people that share the same passion and love for Bruce . . .[the Web site bulletin board is] our home away from home if you will." Attending concerts is likened to "where you can meet and bond with total strangers . . . it is like nothing I have experienced." Another fan says "being in this community is like a neighborhood . . . when someone is in need there's usually a great bunch of folks willing to step up." The fans readily display the depths to which Springsteen has influenced them, and he is credited as such: "we all appreciate that Bruce has enriched our lives to a greater or lesser degree, to a point where people who have not yet 'got Bruce' will never understand." One poster suggested that the word *god* could be substituted for *Bruce* and the sentence would still ring true. Another member of greasylake.org says "I think of the 'Radio Nowhere' lyric, 'trying to make a connection to you' and I think that is what this community is about: human connection . . . TO BE TRULY ALIVE!" Doah expresses his feeling particularly well, using the bible to support his vision:

> Now, outside of Greasy Lake and Springsteen, and the second I saw the word "community" in your post, the very first thing I think of is Acts 2:41–42 and Acts 4:32–37. Those two passages are the most beautiful picture of a community I have ever read with things like, "fellowship," "shared meals," and having things in common. Community, in general, is the best we can be a part of this side of Heaven.

These descriptions leave a distinct impression of a culture presenting members with a distinct identification. Symbols and rituals hold mutually agreed upon meanings and purposes, and explanation is not needed when among one's own kind. "And the multitude of them that believed were of one heart and of one soul: neither said any of them that ought of the things which he possessed was his own; but they had all things in common." (Acts 4:32)

The sense of community among Springsteen fans is strong and across the board taken for granted, much as a member of a religious group takes for granted his or her fellow members' beliefs. This fan society is indeed as inclusive and embracing as any congregation of any denomination (Turner 1982). The relationship between fans, both those who actually meet in the flesh and those who have only a cyber connection, is loosely that of fictive kin: our extended family of chosen individuals, and not kin by means of blood or marriage. We are brothers and sisters in Bruce. And while not all fans or fan-site posters develop these fictive kinships, many do and accept some of the lesser responsibilities that all relationships bring: pleasantries and acknowledgements, emotional support, a ready ear to listen, and shoulder to cry on. One of the important things that Springsteen fans—those active on these "boards"—experience is their shared sense of "getting it." Invariably, this term is always used when discussing the depths-of-feeling Springsteen, his music, and performances elicit. Victor Turner (1982) called this *spontaneous communitas*, this "getting it," and described it as "a flash of lucid mutual understanding on the existential level. When even two people believe that they experience unity, all people are felt by these two, even if only for a flash, to be one" (47–48). In this way, fans relate directly to one another, free of "culturally defined encumbrances" (48). Turner calls communitas the "shared flow" (133), and this is indeed how it feels, an emotion flowing from one fan to another, an electric jolt of mutual understanding. Cultural differences fall away and become inconsequential and language is no barrier. There is something visceral and elemental also about this flash of instant communion, our moment of being "saved."

This "flow" translates into activities as diverse as strangers hugging during a particularly intense musical moment during a show, or in giving what the world outside the fan community would call a "total stranger" a ride to or from a show, and then offering this stranger a place to stay. It is evidenced in the free trading or giving away of concert "bootlegs;" and this good will and shared emotional state ultimately creates the climate for the charity works done around the unifying force of Bruce Springsteen's name.

A more cynical—and hence, less fan-accepted—analysis is that a devotee of any particular cultural commodity is in actuality *not* a member of a real community, but rather a member of a consumption-community; the feeling of community lasts not much past the act of consumption itself (the concert), "and then fades away, which is why we must consume repeatedly" (Joe), to recharge and reaffirm. I feel it necessary here to emphasize that the speaker "Joe" is by his own admission *not* a "fan." His is too simple an explanation, and while it may apply to concert-goers of other groups, the idea of community as an act of consumption does not hold up. Some fans on these Web sites have never seen a concert, only vicariously experiencing a live show through reviews or listening to bootlegs, yet still feel the inclusion of the community. Springsteen fans conduct themselves as a community beyond and outside of the concert-going milieu and spread the good news.

Chapter 6

Listening for the Liberated Word

American religion needs an American voice . . . As Jesus was a man of the people who spoke to them out of the experience of their day-to-day lives and proclaimed justice and freedom even in the midst of oppression—good news to the captive, et cetera—so, too, must we listen for that liberating word in today's vernacular. (Rev. Suzanne Meyer)

A thoughtful and deliberate writer, Springsteen's early lyrics center around themes that are familiar and of concern to many people—belonging, inclusion, freedom, future. These themes transcend age groups, as one teenage fan wrote:

> What I love most about his music is I can hear him tell a story and yeah I've been in that situation, and in some cases take advice he gave back in 1985 and apply [it] to 2004 . . . whenever I hear something in his music that I can relate to it draws me closer to it. (badscooter)

"Converts" see their own experiences reflected in Springsteen's words. His honesty and the hope highlighted in his songs provide members of the "congregation" with the tools—philosophy, philanthropy, compassion—to cope in an increasingly inhospitable and isolating society. Devotees find solace in these songs in much the same way that devoutly practicing religious people find solace in the sacred texts of their religions. A sense of grace, divine virtue, resides in the music. (A retired Baptist minister once told me that justice is getting what we deserve, mercy is not getting what we deserve, and grace is getting what we don't deserve.) There is a Springsteen line appropriate for most any event, and the appropriateness of a particular line might vary for the same person from point to point on the continuum of his or her own life—much like lines from scriptures or poetry.

As mentioned previously, Springsteen describes his music and songs as being "not literally autobiographical . . . but in some way they're emotionally autobiographical . . . some emotional thread you've tried to use to make your own way through what can feel like a particularly imponderable existence" (Primeaux 1996:8, 17). Thus, we, his audience, see reflections of real people. He is obviously not singing about himself but about those people suffering, hurting, and struggling in this "imponderable existence." It is this "empathetic identification," this "reaching out to the other for the other" (Primeaux 1996:96) that the fans respond to, coupled with his apparent authenticity and corresponding behavior. His fans in some fashion trust in his work as a reflection of the man and appreciate his fierce commitment to and trust in his audience (Smith 2002). It is also this identification that leads to the "works of faith" performed by a variety of the initiated, as described in the next chapter. Connecting Mr. Springsteen's music to faith and spirituality is not difficult for one who has listened to his music, and indeed, numerous articles in both the popular press and professional journals by clergy and laypeople alike attest to this. Biblical allusions abound in his lyrics while portraying themes of alienation and community, hope, betrayal, redemption, grace, and generosity. Sermons have been written using his lyrics.

While calling himself a "lapsed-Catholic," Springsteen seems unable—and unwilling—to escape his Catholic upbringing. Christopher Stratton (2007), in his piece "Springsteen and the Minor Prophets," likens Bruce to Micah: both are seeking to imbue a nation with moral guidance, "drawing them back to God" and giving hope back to the people while proclaiming the "culpability of all." Nobody wins unless everybody wins. Stratton may be speaking in hyperbole when he proclaims, by quoting Abraham Joshua Heschel, that Springsteen is one "whose image is our refuge in distress, and whose voice and vision sustain our faith. His red baseball cap and blue jeans are to America what camel's hair and locust were to ancient Israel" (2007). But to his fans, Springsteen does function as a source of both inspiration and solace. And yes, some do apotheosize him. As one fan said, "in the end, the only church that's ever worked for me is the Church of Bruce Springsteen. . . . I don't think he's the Messiah, although he may very well be a Bodhisattiva" (Somerset 2007)—or a boy prophet, walking "handsome and hot" on E Street.

Sowing Seeds of Spirituality: The Covenant

Show a little faith, there's magic in the night ("Thunder Road")

> I know this is idealistic but part of the idea our band had from the begin-
> ning was that you did not have to lose your connection to the people you
> write for. I don't believe that fame or success means that you lose that
> connection, and I don't believe that makin' more money means you lose
> it. Because that's not where the essence of what you are lies. That's not
> what separates people. What separates people are the things that are in
> their heart. So I can just never surrender to that idea. Because I know that
> before I started playing, I was alone. And one of the reasons I picked up
> the guitar was that I wanted to be part of something . . . and I ain't about
> to give it up now. . . . one of the things always on my mind to do was to
> maintain connections with the people I'd grown up with, and the sense of
> community where I came from . . . the danger of fame is in *forgetting*.
> (Springsteen in Marsh 2004:315)

There is little doubt that a Springsteen concert awards the faithful with a
sense of community and communion, if not holiness. This sense of connection that Springsteen mentions in the above quote works to form the basis of
the covenant between Bruce and his fans, to never forget who and where he
came from, and the debt and responsibility he owes his followers: to be honest and "true" to his audience while expecting the same in return. This is also
what creates the intimacy and sense of connection *with* Springsteen.

Springsteen's is an ecumenical congregation, embracing all faiths. While
the imagery in Springsteen's songs is decidedly Christian, and more pointedly
Catholic, the lyrics read in such a way as to be more inclusive should one
choose to look past the Christian images. One long-standing and resolute fan
has written a book, *Greetings from Bury Park*, that details growing up Muslim
in England and how Springsteen played a part in his maturation (Manzoor
2007). Another beloved fan tale tells the "parable" of a young man who met
Bruce in a movie theater and invited him home to meet his parents; this
young man was an Orthodox Jew, wearing the garb of his sect. Bruce accompanied him home after the film and stayed for dinner with his family. The
next day, Bruce left tickets at the box office for his concert that night for
everyone. All are welcome in the Ministry of Rock and Roll, an embracing
and inclusive congregation, the original congregation of reconciliation.

The concert hall serves as Springsteen's divine/sacred space, and he is
able to pass this holiness on to his congregants, the faithful fans gathered for
the "service." George Yamin, in the *Journal of Religious Studies*, says that
Springsteen's music is "nothing less than a modern-day theological epic—
implicitly written in accordance with a single, comprehensive design—in

which Springsteen assimilates and reinterprets, in terms suitable for his listeners, many of the essential ideas of the Hebrew-Christian tradition"
(1983:2). Just as I can no more answer why some people resonate with Christianity and not all religious faiths, I cannot explain why people find this particular rock 'n' roll—and not all—life altering; it is all in what grabs their
attention and snags their soul.

"Rock and roll," says Danny Duncan Collum, "is a communal affair"
(2000:55), and indeed Springsteen and his audience know this. This is the
basis of the covenant Springsteen has implicitly made with his fans: "you be
true to me, and I'll be true to you." He has stated time and again in numerous
interviews that his is a job, and he owes his audience honesty and sincerity, as
well as a damn good rock show. He seems self-reflective enough to realize
and acknowledge that the fans are in part responsible for keeping his creative
impulses flowing. "I think that's what people come for; they want to be lifted
up and grounded at the same time . . . hey, you're not alone, I'm not alone"
(in Graff 2005:xx). When questioned about his absolute complete abandon in
concert and why he seemed to give so much of himself, he answered:

> There may be no tomorrow. . . if you start rationing, you're living life bit
> by bit . . . that's what I get the most satisfaction out of: to know that
> tonight when I go to bed I did my best. If you go to the show, the kid has a
> ticket for tonight. He's got no ticket for the show in L.A. or New York. . . .
> You can't live on what you did yesterday or plan what's gonna happen
> tomorrow. That's what rock 'n' roll is a promise, an oath. It's about being
> as true as you can be at any particular moment. (in Cross 1989:81)

In concert during the *The Ghost of Tom Joad* Tour, a more mature and
older Bruce said:

> Our mission is a search for beauty, and in beauty there is hope, and in
> hope there is some sense of divine love, of faith, of community and possi-
> bility, of things that would combat the brutality and the violence and the
> suffering. That's what I'm trying to lay out there. It's a survival guide.

For many of his faithful, his music is exactly that—a survival guide fed on
divine love. "I believe in the love that you gave me, I believe in the faith that
can save me, I believe in the hope and I pray that someday it may raise me
above these badlands" (Springsteen 2003:71)—these words could be as easily
directed to his God as well as his audience. And the audience responds as
joyously as any congregation responding to the Gospel or any other sacred
text or hymn, and as physically as any Sufi dancer-poet or whirling dervish.

One group of dedicated fans from Northern California refers to itself,
with more than a little seriousness, as the "Church of Bruce" (Sanders 2008),
a term echoed in other fan communities. "Bruce feeds my soul . . . it's like a

religion, you just can't explain it," says one fan, while another says "He gives us hope love and faith . . . it's like church. I get spiritually uplifted" (Sanders 2008). The terms used by many fans when describing their Springsteen connection are hyperbolic, such as transformative, life changing, redemptive, and others that usually are associated with a deeply religious experience.

Good News, Good Works

As with any congregation, fans join together in times of need or pleasure. Of no small significance is the way in which fans unite to help each other out. One of the members of the group mentioned above fell on hard times recently, losing health, employment, and housing. The group, unknown to this person, took up a collection and presented fan x with a sizeable check to help defray living expenses. And some years ago, on the official Sony Springsteen Web site now lost to the Ethernet, brucespringsteen.net, one California fan was made homeless and jobless as a result of the devastating wildfires that had spread through Southern California. She posted her plight, and the members of a forum thread called "Tramps Like Us" took up a collection and sent money and food, as well as catnip and cat food for the fan's cat, to help her through those hard times. This same group of fans also managed to get a Christmas tree and presents to a single-mom fan who had recently lost her home and job. Other fans collect toiletries to send to military personnel in Iraq, while maintaining a neutral position on the war itself. These supply drives and charitable collections represent the equivalent of the passing of the collection plate in other houses of worship.

And the clergy is represented among the Springsteen faithful also. Reverend B is a 44-year-old senior minister at a Methodist church in North Carolina. A graduate of a Kentucky Baptist Divinity School, he chose to leave the Baptist church and become a Methodist minister after what he called a "fundamentalist takeover." He and his wife have been Springsteen fans for over 30 years and have seen any number of live shows. As mentioned previously in chapter 2, Reverend B designed a series of sermons and services crafted around the songs of Bruce Springsteen. His church offers two services on Sundays: a 9:00 AM "contemporary" service, complete with a rock ensemble made up of congregation members, and an 11:00 AM service that he termed "more traditional." He has no qualms about conducting the 9:00 AM services, but says he is carefully weighing how to present the Springsteen songs to his less change-receptive audience at his 11:00 AM service. I asked him if he felt any misgivings about using contemporary rock songs within the context of his religious service, and he replied, "Not at all. Bruce speaks to the human condition that we all experience; I will just need to present it more carefully at my later service."

Reverend B also believes that the music connects to "something deeper." This plays into the supposition posited by Gordon Lynch that there is a longing felt by many people for a spirituality that is "liberated from the certainties of the institutional church," and who are looking for spiritual inspiration, for want of a better term, from someone who is more like themselves, someone with whom they can more readily identify (Lynch 2004:163). The idea that a Springsteen concert can closely resemble a religious service—albeit a high-spirited one—did not seem like a foreign idea to Reverend B. I asked him why he chose Springsteen, and he replied because the music was fairly popular and referenced spiritual things in the lyrics. In the past, he has constructed sermons and services around other music and, given Bruce's scheduled appearance in April, he decided that now was the proper time for Springsteen. Reverend B, who has a long-standing familiarity and love of Springsteen's music, took his then 17-year-old son with him to see *The Rising* Tour in Greensboro on December 8, 2002, and called it "one of the best nights I had with my teenager. When he went into 'The Rising' my son turned to me and said 'Dad, I've never seen anything so amazing!'" He went on to speak about the healing that this particular tour and album provided for many fans after the horrific events of September 11, 2001. Reverend B was so taken with the performance and the emotional fulfillment it provided that he went to see another show in Chapel Hill the following spring. This is a repeated pattern among Springsteen fans, the need to see multiple shows on any given tour, akin to attending church services to renew and maintain faith, constantly "going to the well" for renewal.

The reverend also spoke about the shared—actual or assumed—character of mutual fans, and the trust this shared musical experience creates, echoing opinions of other fans with whom I've spoken. Many devotees see a deeper meaning in their musical experience, citing the stimulus to "never sit back . . . always remember that we are here for others, not just for ourselves. And I think that's also a basic tenet of religion. I do good things because it's the right thing to do . . . and I think that is a core of many songs" (LOFG). One practicing, deeply Christian fan told me:

> I realize that the joyful exuberance I feel at a Bruce Springsteen concert is God-given, just as Bruce's creative genius and masterful performing skills are God-given. Just as I am made up of body, soul, and spirit in a way I can't explain, but know to be true, Bruce's songs connect with my spirit and thereby enrich my life. My life has followed the wonderful, fulfilling, surprising path that God, in His wisdom, has laid out for me. In some mysterious, unnamable fashion, Bruce Springsteen, the man, and his

music has accompanied me along the journey. Perhaps that is why our creator God who made us in His image gave us the gift of art. I cannot imagine my life without the art of Bruce Springsteen. (jj)

This ineffable quality again repeats in fans' descriptions of what they hear and feel both in and through Springsteen's music. (It is of interest to note here that the above quoted person is the mother of five and not your typical rock and roll fan—if there even is such a creature.) Other fans talk about Springsteen's songs as "God speaking directly to me through these words" (hanaree), or connecting them to "a better/higher realization and recognition" (yark). Hardgirloneasystreet says: "I was truly in the church of Bruce. I believe that some people are put on this earth to unite us, move us, fill us with joy. That is Bruce." Blueguitar had this to say about a recent show:

> He [Bruce] made his case for fighting back against the squalor with nothing but sweat drenched desire, his own personal fight to open the door and let people dance away their own demons with a physically demanding show that was touched with the stirring intellectuality and spiritual hope, all in the guise of a rock and roll show. . . . Bruce used the echo and call to get them [the audience] to respond to him. . . . Bruce sang, "It's all right, it's all right, it's all right," and the audience threw up their hands and yelled back "yeah," a positive confirmation to counter this world of pain and negativity.

It is expected in concert, this response, when Bruce calls, and fans enact their part of the service well. We wave our arms and pump our fists, we sing louder when Bruce challenges us with a "I can't hear you" or a finger to his ear, singing back to him our parts in joyous unison. Yes, we say to him with our actions and voices, there *is* somebody alive out here! We are alive, and we celebrate you even as you celebrate us. In concert, Bruce can take his audience from "hell to this blessed life . . . in the spiritual Church of Springsteen . . . the only redemption that matters is the 'Beat of your heart, the beat of your heart, the beat of your heart'" (blueguitar).

The Reverend Suzanne Meyer, a Unitarian minister who saw Springsteen as "America's religious voice," had also fashioned a service and sermon around Bruce Springsteen (see chapter 2). In a personal e-mail, she stated that, as she said, the author "of a new gospel is anyone who has the courage and conviction to step out of the crowd and speak the truth," and she saw Springsteen as one of these messengers.

The desire to introduce family and friends to the experience of Springsteen's live shows and to share the emotional and spiritual connection is another common trait of the Springsteen fan community—much as it is of any religious community/family. While "finding" Bruce may have been a solitary and individual experience similar to the Protestant "born again" conversion (Cavicchi

1998:43), the "convert," now imbued with such joy, wishes to share it by converting others who are not yet fans. This evangelism afflicts many members of E Street nation. Every fan I have spoken with has related the experience of taking a close friend or loved one to a show in the hopes that lightening will strike, the uninitiated's eyes will be opened, and another fan will be possessed with the joy, thereby becoming converted. In particular, many parents take their children in the hopes of creating that bridge of communication music can provide and facilitating their "conversion." I have met families of three generations of Springsteen fans at shows: Mom H brought both her 80-plus-year-old mother and teenage daughter to a 2003 show in Boston. It is a common sight to see families in the audience with children of all ages. While in France to attend a concert in 2007, I met a family from the United States—Mom, Dad, and three pre-teen and teenaged children attempting to obtain tickets to the Springsteen show in Paris. All of these children knew the music and the history. Much like the joy that is found in a newly embraced religious belief, sharing Bruce and watching the convert "get it" creates a feeling of sanctity and holy gratitude.

At shows and preshow gatherings, the devoted fans who have traveled for hundreds or thousands of miles meet and mingle with new fans and the unconverted. The older fans who have seen more shows and traveled more miles serve as witnesses for Bruce, establishing their own particular set of reasons for traveling so far or for having seen so many concerts. The unconverted listen, and after the show, they often profess their new-found faith in the ministry of Bruce. This faith is reinforced and nurtured by the community via cyber involvement on the various Web sites.

Chapter 7

Spirit in the Night

Good News through Social Justice

And remember, nobody wins unless everybody wins.
(Bruce Springsteen)

Ye shall know them by their fruits. (Matthew 7:16)

On September 20, 1981, Bruce played a sold-out concert in Los Angeles, with all the proceeds going to the Vietnam Veterans Association, raising over a quarter of a million dollars: "Without Bruce and that evening, we would not have made it, we would have had to close down" said then-VVA president Bob Muller (in Marsh 2004:310). At the beginning of that night's performance, Muller took the stage and addressed the audience. One particularly poignant section of speech talked about the lack of help that the Vietnam vets were getting from the government or private industry:

> It's a little bit ironic that for the years that we've been tryin', when the businesses haven't come behind us and the political leaders have failed to rally behind us that, when you remember the divisions within our own generation about the war, it ultimately turns out to be the very symbol of our generation—rock and roll!—that brings us together. And it is rock and roll that is going to provide the healing process that everybody needs. (in Marsh 2004:313)

Without Springsteen, Muller says, there would have been no Vietnam veterans movement. This benefit was one of the initial examples of the *"nobody*

75

wins unless everybody wins" tenet that was an often-spoken line by Bruce while onstage during the mid- to late-eighties; it was the Springsteen equivalent of the Golden Rule, frequently repeated by his fans, and one he seems to take to heart. This line may also reflect a literal manifestation of what Bruce was— and still is—doing behind the scenes, and away from tabloids and the public eye. Springsteen has been privately and without fanfare supporting a number of charitable organizations over the past several decades.

Prior to 1984, Springsteen and the E Street Band, or Springsteen performing solo, had appeared at several big-name rock and roll benefits. The near-catastrophic disaster at Pennsylvania's Three Mile Island prompted a group of West Coast musicians to form MUSE—Musicians United for Safe Energy—and to organize an all-star fund-raiser at Madison Square Garden in New York City in late 1979 that came to be known, via album and video, as No Nukes (Marsh 2004). While No Nukes was a moderate success, it was the Vietnam vets benefit that seems to have been the real spiritual turning point for Bruce. In an interview with *Rolling Stone Magazine* writer Kurt Loder, Springsteen said:

> I want to try and just work more directly with people, try to find some way that my band can tie into the communities that we come into . . . human politics. I think that people on their own can do a lot. . . . Where do the aesthetic issues that you write about intersect with some sort of concrete action, some direct involvement in the communities that your audience comes from? (in Marsh 2004:489)

Springsteen and his management team began to search for groups around the country that benefited "the hungry, the homeless, and the unemployed" (Marsh 2004:489).

Dating back decades, Springsteen has been donating to and working with charities all over the world. Originally, I intended to include a partial list of charities and organizations to which Bruce was a known contributor as an appendix to this book. It was, however, asked that this list not be included. This is much in keeping with the man's character and his penchant for flying below the radar in his private life, and as such, I must respect that. What this does, however, is make it difficult for this writer to factually document the information that follows. Where possible, I will cite the sources of my information, but much of what I am about to relate comes from the Internet community and newspapers. The upshot of my research is that Bruce Springsteen has always put his money where his mouth is—literally and figuratively. He has a reputation along the Jersey Shore of being generous and engaged with his community, apparently well deserved and earned.

The Web site looktothestars.org lists, in their "charity biography" for Springsteen, the following organizations with which he has a connection:

Amnesty International, Hudson River Sloop Clearwater, Kristen Ann Carr Fund, Musicians on Call, Project Greenleaf, Rainforest Foundation Fund, and World Hunger Year. Most of the groups Springsteen supports, aside from those actively engaged in research for specific purposes, reflect his awareness of and concerns about events and issues affecting everyday life. Descriptions of these funds can be accessed through the above Web site. Also listed on this celebrity-watching site are listings of ticket auctions where Springsteen has donated concert tickets and meet-and-greets in the E Street Lounge, a "backstage" bar-type reception open to only those with special access passes, to be auctioned off to benefit one organization or another. But there are also many, many recipients of Springsteen's generosity not listed on this site.

A 1996 article in the New Jersey *Star-Ledger* by Suna Chang ("Putting His Money") lists a number of beneficiaries of Springsteen largesse. In 1993, World Hunger Year received $200,000 from a benefit performance at the Meadowlands. In October of that same year, Springsteen held a benefit at the grammar school he attended in Freehold, New Jersey, while three November Springsteen benefit performances at the Paramount Theater in Asbury Park generated funds for The Boys and Girls Club of Monmouth County, the Women's Center of Monmouth County, and the Asbury Park Fire Department. According to Rose Mikolon, development director of the Women's Center, an anonymous Springsteen fan gave $50,000 to the center following the concert (BC). The fire department used the money to buy sorely needed equipment: "We were in need of new equipment so the chief here just wrote to Springsteen," said Fire Inspector Jim Bruno. "The men didn't even know (about the letter) until we got the response. We didn't want to get their hopes up." Some of this money was used to replace an outdated extrication device commonly known as the "jaws of life" (BC).

More recently, in November of 2009, Bruce made a pledge to the Second Harvest Food Bank of Charlotte, North Carolina, to match dollar for dollar any donation between $10,000 and $50,000. The Springs Close Foundation of York County donated $50,000, and Springsteen matched this gift with his own check for $50,000. "We've been told that Bruce Springsteen likes to do things like this under the radar, without much publicity, so not many people knew about it in advance," said Springs Close Foundation President Angela McCrae (Price 2009).

This was done without fanfare and publicity, and to this day, it is difficult tracking all of Springsteen's charitable donations. In each city he has visited, he has met with local groups, expressing his "concern for depressed conditions" in the communities, and presented them with a significant donation; there was a stipulation included with the donation, though, that the organization wait until after the first show to discuss the contribution (Marsh 2004).

When asked by the press why he chose not to make a statement, his assistant Barbara Carr replied, "This *is* his statement" (in Marsh 2003:498). Around this time, he began making announcements from the stage encouraging his fans to get involved, either through donations or by working with the organizations. At a show in Syracuse, New York, he asked if anyone in the audience could donate a forklift to the new Food Bank of Central New York; within a week, someone did just that (Marsh 2004). A favorite cause, and one that he still actively supports, was eradicating hunger, and the local food banks and representatives were invited to collect donations at each performance; tickets also were provided to be auctioned off, with the proceeds going to the food bank. These organizations helped the people that Bruce most related to, people who must have reminded him of his childhood and what his life could have been.

These charitable connections happened—and continue to happen—in each and every city visited, and every country as well. In England, Springsteen contributed to a local miners' union strike fund, donating some £16,000 to the Miners' Wives Support Group. In Australia, he donated to the Children's Hospital/Youth Ward, the Prince Alexander Hospital Transplant Trust Fund, and the Vietnam Veterans Association of Australia. In Japan, Springsteen's people had to dig hard to find an appropriate social organization, as food banks did not exist there; so, he donated to a fund that helped "unmarriageable widows of men who had died in traffic accidents" (Marsh 2004:530). In Clifton, Arizona, Springsteen provided the means to keep the People's Clinic open in a town ravaged by a years-long copper miners' strike. Days away from closing, Bruce's donation enabled the clinic to move to a better facility and remain open (Marsh 2004). In Los Angeles County, he visited the union hall for steelworkers' Local 1845 and participated in a theater workshop, leaving concert tickets for the union members (Marsh 2004).

For Springsteen, the American Dream "ain't about two cars in the garage. It's about people living and working together without steppin' on each other" (in Marsh 2004:503–04). He literally put his money where his mouth was to the tune of $10,000 to $25,000, depending on the venue (Marsh 2004). He continues to do this today, supporting the Second Harvest Food Banks as well as the Community for Fairness and Dignity for the Homeless and the National Union for the Homeless, among other causes. A minister in North Carolina told me that each time Springsteen plays in the state, he donates $10,000 to the Christian Urban Ministry—but I was unable to verify this. It is policy apparently in the Springsteen management organization to decline to talk about what Bruce must see as a private matter. Likewise, many of those organizations benefitting from his interest remain close-mouthed and do not respond to questions regarding his donations.

But Springsteen's contributions are not restricted to organizations. In 1999, 23-year-old Amadou Diallo was shot 41 times in a case of mistaken identity by New York City police. Springsteen wrote a song about this tragedy, and it was played for the first time in concert on The Reunion Tour. Aptly entitled "American Skin (41 Shots)," when the E Street Band performed ten nights in New York City, Diallo's mother, Kadiatou Diallo, was invited to one of the shows and escorted backstage to meet Bruce. Ms. Diallo revealed to Meg Guroff, Jim Jerome, and Lyndon Stambler (2009:72) in the September/October 2009 edition of the *AARP Magazine* that:

> I never expected to hear from him after that. But he did something that I have never shared with the public. He sent us pictures that he took with us, and he donated money in Amadou's honor for scholarships at four colleges in New York City.

The best leaders lead by example, and Bruce has set the bar high; fans see his efforts to contribute to change and feel inspired to do so themselves—maybe not all fans, and not to the extent that Bruce does, but we try and do what we can. "Nobody wins unless everybody wins."

More recently, it appears that Springsteen's interest in, and support of, local food growing initiatives has been increasing. At a show in Rochester, New York (March 6, 2007), an organization called Rochester Roots had representatives collecting donations in the arena. When I approached a worker and attempted to find out if Bruce had made a monetary donation, the worker quite politely told me that she was not free to give me that information, consistent with Springsteen policy. This organization, according to their literature, is committed to creating a local and sustainable food system that is "nutritionally, ecologically, and economically sound" through education, advocacy, and community development. They also run a school community garden project, turning underutilized schoolyards into urban gardens; at present, they work with three local elementary schools located in areas of Rochester "where food insecurity is high" (www.rochesterroots.org).

In the same vein, through a mutual colleague, I learned that Springsteen's organization had made contact with a Greensboro grassroots group related to the University of North Carolina–Greensboro campus. Called Project Greenleaf (greenleaf.uncg.edu) and supporting local and sustainable agriculture, it is a similar type of program as the Rochester organization. Greenleaf's Web site states:

> The mission of Project Green Leaf is to promote and support a local agro-food system. Project Green Leaf is dedicated to sustaining local agriculture by strengthening community between farmers and consumers, thus providing for better quality of living.

By promoting various activities, such as direct marketing and educational/outreach programs, we assist in developing the connections necessary for a local agro-food system.

According to Project Greenleaf's founder, the group was approached and asked if they would be interested in collecting money at Springsteen's Greensboro concert. The Springsteen representative who made contact stated that Greenleaf was "the wave of the future." These initiatives are in line philosophically with the organizations in which Bruce has historically been interested, organizations that allow people to help themselves. I also learned that he had made a large donation to the group, yet when I approached the volunteers collecting at the arena, they coyly answered my questions by neither denying nor confirming my information.

The concept of and belief in community runs all through Springsteen's music, and it becomes important to look at the communities from which Springsteen came, and the ways in which he has acknowledged and honored them. Just down the road from Asbury Park is Freehold, New Jersey, Springsteen's birthplace. Signs of Springsteen, though, are virtually nonexistent. There are no signs saying "Springsteen slept here," no gated home á la Graceland, home of Elvis Presley. Instead of exploiting the "Springsteen connection," the town seems to guard his image and privacy. No street signs advertise his connection to the town, although the streets signs at the corner of E Street and Tenth Avenue have had to be replaced with posts five-or-so feet high, and planted firmly in the ground, because of the too frequent theft of the old street signs. A former mayor, Michael Wilson, says that the town is sensitive to "overblowing" the fact of Springsteen's birth there. Townspeople seem to be protective of his privacy and do not readily answer questions about Bruce. His generosity is felt here, though.

In 1985, the 3M Company announced plans to close its Freehold, New Jersey, plant. The workers decided to reach out to entertainers for help, since the plant made video and audio tapes. Bruce donated $25,000 for the union to place a full-page ad in a national newspaper asking for help. In January 1986, a benefit was held at the Stone Pony in Asbury, and Springsteen showed up to perform. "He propelled the fight into a totally different arena," said worker Stan Fischer (Chang 1996). Springsteen continued donating to the workers' cause, giving another $25,000 to an organization called Hometowns against Shutdowns, now defunct. In 1987, he was responsible for making it possible for the play "Lady Beth," written and performed by unemployed steelworkers, to be performed at the Stone Pony (Chang 1996).

In 1996, he played a benefit concert for his old school, St. Rose of Lima, to help build a new parish center to serve Freehold's growing Latino population (Hyman 2000). Springsteen also donated $100,000 to the Freehold Fire

Department for the purchase of a new fire engine; stenciled on the side of the engine are the words "Born To Run." The fire department now sells tee shirts with these words, for fund-raising (personal purchase). In return for his philanthropy, the town protects its famous son, apparently acceding to Springsteen's own wishes: no signs, no statues, no sculptures, no streets, and no parks bear his name (Hyman 2000). In spite of the fact that Springsteen is a self-admitted "attention whore," he presents a demure persona, avoiding any publicity surrounding his charitable acts and maintaining his humble posture of an average working-class father and family man; average and working class, in actuality, he is not.

Just a few scant miles north up the beach is Asbury Park. Asbury Park has always held a special place in the hearts of Springsteen fans. Once a thriving beach community, time has not been kind to the town or its residents. All "real" fans know the stories of Bruce and Asbury Park, know about the clubs where Springsteen played, know the story of Bruce meeting Clarence.

Most fans who come to New Jersey make the pilgrimage to Asbury and Freehold to see for themselves the places mentioned in song—E Street and Tenth Avenue in Freehold, the Palace, the boardwalk, Madame Marie's in Asbury Park, and so on. Springsteen's first album was entitled *Greetings from Asbury Park,* and featured a postcard-like image on the front cover. His second album *The Wild, The Innocent, and The E Street Shuffle,* with songs like "Fourth of July" and "Asbury Park (Sandy)," forever immortalized the fortune-telling skills of Madame Marie and the boardwalk where she practiced her art. Fans come from all over the world to have their pictures taken in front of the modest, tiny building that today still houses Madame Marie's business. Madame Marie passed away in 2008, but the business is still open, and now run by her son and daughter . . . and yes, I did have my fortune told by Madame Marie before she died.

Asbury Park has been in decline since World War II, and the opening of the Garden State Parkway sealed its fate. In its heyday, Asbury supported over 200 hotels with as many as 600,000 tourists a season coming to walk on its boardwalk and sun on its beaches. But the only constant is change, and with the opening of the Garden State Parkway, tourism expanded down the coast. Race riots on July 4, 1970, resulted in the destruction of a five-block area on the west side of Asbury and over 100 injuries. The middle class scampered away, leaving Asbury to a legacy of corruption and political mismanagement that exists to this day.

The advent of gambling in Atlantic City, 60-plus miles south down the Jersey shore, drove the city further out of the tourism market (Lindberg 2009). In 2004, Asbury ranked only below Camden and Irvington on the state's most dangerous city list. According to the U.S. Census Bureau, the city covers 1.6 square miles, 1.3 of which are land. There are 23 known gangs in Asbury Park; in the 1999–2000 school year, suspension rates at the middle and high school hovered around 48 percent of enrolled students. Not surprisingly, as with other places where poverty is rampant, Asbury Park has the lowest graduation rate in the state, the highest state HIV and STD rates, and the highest teen pregnancy rate. (I was unable to verify accurately all of these figures, but my source says that these figures, from 2001, came from a city official who handed a paper entitled "City of Asbury Park, Profiles and Social Indicators" to him at a business meeting.) Situated in Monmouth County, one of New Jersey's wealthiest counties, the per capita Asbury income in 2000 was $13,516, with 30.1 percent of the population living below the poverty line.

The 2002 Springsteen song, "My City of Ruins" was written about Asbury Park, and yet was appropriate when sung at the 9/11 telethon to raise money for survivors of that tragedy. Whatever his reasons, Springsteen remains emotionally attached to the area in some fashion. Asbury Park and his own personal story of growing up have assuredly contributed to his desire to aid the town and its citizens. In spite of the bleak numbers mentioned above, a recent e-mail correspondence from a friend noted that there is no city this size as well-known or romantically perceived. His e-mail went on to state: "It can fairly be argued that the impact of Bruce's Asbury Park lyrics, his use of Asbury photos on tour memorabilia and record sleeves, and the love he's bestowed upon the community has had a far greater impact than all of his financial contributions to local organizations, combined" (pbjcrane, e-mail received 12/14/09). This friend continued, saying that for many years, fans from outside the area traveling to Asbury and spending their money in the town were a critical aid to the community's ability to scrape by, and he calls Springsteen one of the city's biggest boosters. Yet, it is unclear whether or not the bulk of the inhabitants of Asbury Park even realize what a benefactor Springsteen has been, how involved he has been with the community, or if they even appreciate what he has done. BC calls him an "enabler"—not in the traditionally negative, 12-step way in which we customarily understand the term. Bruce donates to organizations to strengthen the organization's ability to reach its goals, to *enable* these groups to help; in other words, rather than feed the hungry, he supports food banks. One might say that he facilitates the activities of each of these groups.

These descriptions and statistics are only an attempt to convey a flavor of what the area is like and to situate the impact a benefactor such as Springsteen can have on an area. His activism and involvement also serve to set an example that many of his fans follow, volunteering in food banks, organizing personal-care-items drives for military men and women stationed in Iraq and

Afghanistan, volunteering with Habitat for Humanity, and any number of other good works.

In December 2003, I attended two of three scheduled Christmas shows at the Convention Hall on the boardwalk in Asbury Park. Tickets were $100 each, and the proceeds of the ticket sales as well as tee-shirt sales went to various Asbury Park venues. Bruce rattled off a list of recipients, too fast for me to catch them all, but one that I did note was a donation to purchase instruments and costumes for the Asbury Park High School marching band. That holiday season, and another in December 2004, saw a promotion of the town of Asbury Park itself; if you purchased merchandise at specific shops and signed up for a drawing, you stood a chance of winning free tickets to the Christmas shows. This brought much needed extra revenue into the city and helped the local shop owners as well.

Prior to every tour in the past decade, Springsteen has held rehearsal shows in Asbury Park, either at the Convention Hall or the Paramount Theater. These are true rehearsal shows, with songs stopped and started, a musical line polished here or there, and can sometimes be a little rough around the edges, performance-wise. But fans vie as avidly for these tickets, also $100 a seat, as with any other Springsteen show. All proceeds from these rehearsal shows are also donated to charity. The Asbury Park Library benefited from these Christmas shows indirectly because of Bruce Springsteen: a library staff member helped a fan secure tickets to these shows, and the fan made a $75,000 donation to the library as a result. Even for Springsteen fans, this is an exceptional donation (BC).

An organization that has always been—as stated previously—near and dear to Bruce's heart is the Community Food Bank of New Jersey. At a session at the *Glory Days Springsteen Symposium* in September of 2009 (described in chapter 2), executive director Kathleen DiChiara spoke about his involvement. "We've never really approached [Springsteen] and asked for help," DiChiara said. "He has always initiated it . . . he's just an extremely generous person. We've had a long history of help from him. I have always said, 'In our darkest hour, Bruce has been there for us.'" She told a story about the food bank moving into a new building in 1987, when the roof on the building collapsed. On Christmas Eve, she received an Express Mail package; it contained a check for $50,000 from Bruce. DiChiara also made a point of telling the session attendees that Springsteen's contributions were not limited to just financial. She told the story of Springsteen showing up on a cold February day in a beat up old car, dressed for the weather and ready to work; he spent the day at the warehouse loading and unloading trucks and taking orders. He is, she says, there for the long haul.

An August 11, 1999, article in the New Jersey *Star-Ledger* speaks about an organization called The Foundation that listed Bruce Springsteen as the president and sole benefactor. According to the article, Springsteen donated at least $350,845 to families in need in the four-year period between 1995 and 1999, verified by the IRS, and continues to contribute $100,000 a year (Drucker 1999). Said Jim McDuffie, the executive director of the then 11-year-old organization, "We've always kept a pretty low profile." (A recent Web search turned up no listings online for this organization, and no references to any group of this name in the area.) The foundation did such things as home repairs for low-income families and replacing heating systems and windows, and operated through word of mouth via churches, civic groups, and the Monmouth County Department of Social Services (Drucker 1999). Then Freehold Mayor Mike Wilson, who grew up with Springsteen and once played in a band with him, said, "I think he remembers where he came from. We grew up pretty much middle class, lower-middle class. Now that he's struck it big, I think he wants to give back" (Drucker 1999). The article goes on to detail help received and thanks given for work done; rotting window frames replaced, new furnaces, new flooring for a wheelchair-bound recipient. And none of these people were aware of the man behind the scenes who made the work possible.

During the *Born in the U.S.A.* Tour, Springsteen donated $10,000 to the Committee for Dignity and Fairness to the Homeless, enabling them to renovate a house in Camden, New Jersey, and to train organizers in other cities (Marsh 2004). Springsteen said from the stage in Philadelphia:

> The Committee was started by homeless people who try to let other homeless people be productive members of society. Right now, they need all the help they can get. The things I'm singing about in my songs are things happening in your everyday life. In a country as rich as ours, it's a shame that fifteen percent of the population live below the poverty level. There's absolutely no reason for it, but it affects all of us. (in Marsh 2004:379)

Why does any of this matter? It matters because this behavior and compassion serves as model conduct for Springsteen fans all over the world. Without Springsteen's generosity, perhaps the Asbury Library wouldn't have gotten its large Christmas donation from a fan ($75,000), or the $50,000 donation to the Monmouth County Women's Center might have never been given. Nobody wins unless everybody wins. What is interesting is that, with African Americans comprising slightly over 62 percent of this New Jersey–area population, it is likely that there are many residents who do not even know who Bruce Springsteen is, as his audience has always been predominately white and, at least now, predominantly affluent. Bruce obviously knows that poverty and need jump all barriers—racial, ethnic, and cultural—and honors the *humanity* of those in need. Equally obvious is that he has no need to be thanked or recognized for his contributions.

Asbury Park is also home to the largest collection of Springsteen items, second only to "my mother's basement" (Springsteen Christmas show, 12/08/01). With over 10,700 holdings, dating back to 1964, the Springsteen Special Collections began as a conversation between two fans—Chris Phillips, the man behind the fan magazine *Backstreets* as well as the Web site backstreets.com, and his friend Bob Crane. In an effort to archive reviews of Springsteen's performances, they put out a call to fans, asking for assistance collecting any documents of interest. Before long, items began rolling into the Backstreets office at such pace and in such volume that Chris and Bob decided to compile the materials as a Special Collection. Currently, it is housed in the Asbury Park Public Library and treated much as any special collection—no material can be removed from the collection, the equivalent of a rare books room (Cirrincione 2003). In 2004, Friends of the Bruce Springsteen Collection was founded, a "not-for-profit organization for people interested in supporting this Collection, and thereby helping to preserve the written history of Bruce Springsteen and his bands" (www.asburyparklibrary.org). Donations are tax deductible.

In addition to the food bank donations all over the country, Springsteen also gives freely of his services in diverse settings and for diverse reasons. He has performed benefits to keep a struggling magazine afloat (Pulitzer prize winning author Walker Percy's *Double Take*, which, despite Bruce's generosity is no longer afloat); to buy uniforms and instruments for the Asbury Park High School marching band; to buy emergency medical equipment for the local rescue squad (Christmas shows); for his children's school (Rumson County Day School); for the Light of Day foundation, which funds Parkinson's Disease research; and for the Kristen Ann Carr Sarcoma Fund; as well as a fund-raiser in Pittsburg after floods there in 2004. Rarely in recent years has Bruce appeared at the more celebrity-laden charity events, with a few exceptions. These include the Tribute to Heroes telethon on September 21, 2001, to benefit the victims and families affected by the World Trade Center disaster, and the Hope for Haiti telethon held to raise money for disaster relief after the January 12, 2009, 7.0 earthquake there. Another cause he has performed for is the Stand Up for Heroes benefits for the Bob Woodruff Foundation, whose aim is to help wounded soldiers and their families to reintegrate into their communities "so they may thrive physically, psychologically, socially and economically" (www.remind.org/about_us).

This idea of sharing the best of ourselves, to help "everybody win," can be seen in the number of charitable events and organizations organized *in* Springsteen's name. One such site is run by the Orel family who also host a Web site with many different kinds of Springsteen trivia and information (www.matt.orel.ws/index.html). But additionally, the Orel family has made an arrangement with the Web site amazon.com to act as a portal to Amazon. Any purchases made by using the Orel link to Amazon result in a commission that the Orel family then matches and donates to a charity favored by Bruce Springsteen. For the first three quarters of 2007, this family distributed $265 to three different charities. While not a fortune, this nevertheless shows the depth of impact Springsteen has had on one family and how they are responding. You can also read reviews of some of the several dozen shows that Matt, the webmaster and involved Springsteen fan, has attended.

Dedicated fans following Springsteen's example have organized and made sizable donations to a number of charities. Prior to a recent show in Buffalo, New York, members of the Web site backstreets.com organized a preshow party. Fans signing up for the party paid ten dollars, and this got them a name tag with their screen name on it, along with assorted appetizers. People had donated a variety of items to be raffled off, and the proceeds of this raffle, along with the ten-dollar fees minus the restaurant bill, were donated to the Western New York branch of Second Harvest Food Bank—some $500.

As mentioned previously, at a 2003 show, I was able to collect nearly $3,000 in a matter of minutes at a tailgate party of another Web site, greasy-lake.org. Recently, backstreets.com members sponsored a women's build day at a Habitat for Humanity site in New Jersey; 20 women signed up to help build this house, the maximum number of volunteers Habitat can handle in any given day. While some of the women were acquaintances or friends, others, like my daughter and I, knew only each other and perhaps one other worker. We insulated walls and ceilings that day, a nasty, dirty job, but there were no complaints to be heard. By the end of the day, we were part of the group and no longer among strangers.

One of the most ambitious of the fan initiatives is the "Bruce Sent Me" campaign (http://brucesentme.com). To quote from the Web site,

> The idea is to demonstrate in a tangible way what a difference the music we love can make in the world. . . . "WITH THESE HANDS" we are making a difference.
>
> Bruce Sent Me is not interested in collecting your money. We simply want to inspire you to share and to look out for those less fortunate. We were moved by Bruce's encouragement to "rise up" and we are simply here to pass that thought along. Although Bruce Springsteen is not affiliated in any way with Bruce Sent Me (if you're looking for his official site, a link is provided below), we'd like to believe he approves of the way we heeded his advice. If you feel it too, please share this idea with others in any way you feel comfortable. To borrow a phrase from the Boss, "Turn it up!" (note: "Turn it up" is a line from "Mary's Place")

The idea for Bruce Sent Me had its birth in a posting on the fan site backstreets.com, encouraging fans to heed Bruce's evening "public service announcement" as he called it, and donate to suggested charities. Within days, thousands of dollars were raised (www.brucesentme.com). Were it not for the concerned spirit of Bruce himself, it is doubtful that this site would exist. Shortly after its inception and just prior to Thanksgiving, the only refrigerated truck owned by the Community Food Bank of New Jersey was involved in an accident on the New Jersey Turnpike, losing its entire shipment of 2,000 turkeys targeted for needy families. Within a week, Bruce Sent Me raised $6,000 to assist in the replacement of the truck and the Thanksgiving turkeys (Strauss 2003). (As mentioned previously, Bruce himself has been known to simply drop in to the warehouse of the food bank to help unload trucks.) Links on the Bruce Sent Me site took one directly to America's Second Harvest Food Banks Web site, where the food bank arranged that donations could be acknowledged as Bruce Sent Me donations (secondharvest.org/how_to_help/Bruce_Sent_Me.html).

What, really, can be more spiritual than doing "good works," to treat each human being with the dignity and respect awarded them by the Creator? Words come cheaply, but actions again can be love made manifest. These deeds are all a direct result of fans being touched by Bruce's music and, more pointedly, his humanity and compassion; this is a tangible way for fans to honor their avatar. Without his example, likely most of this fan-sponsored altruism would not take place.

And faith *will* be rewarded sometimes: on July 31, 2004, during a Habitat for Humanity work day organized by btxers, as members of the Web site backstreets.com are called, Bruce himself showed up to share pizza and beers at the end of the day (Celano 2004). Whether by word, music, or deed, Bruce serves as a moral compass for his followers, reminding us that we are, indeed, our brothers' keepers, and we are all out here on this road together.

Chapter 8

Witness for Bruce

I'll work for your love, dear
I'll work for your love
("I'll Work For Your Love")

To understand the emotional depths of fan involvement in the community, both actual and virtual, it is best to hear what fans have to say themselves, to hear their "witnessing" and conversion stories as they tell them in their own words. The stories all have a familiar ring and progression: alone, hearing a song that strikes a chord, experiencing a sudden epiphany and realization of joy—again, not unlike my experience being "saved" at a Billy Graham crusade. And this also feeds into the sense of shared experience, knowing that other fans have felt this way, have been hit by the same bolt of Springsteen. The only identification used for these stories are screen names used on Internet bulletin boards. Some of these stories deserve to be told in full, while others will be excerpted. The names used are the screen names used online.

> **SpringsteenMagic:**
> When I was born, my parents—especially my father—were huge Bruce fans. I grew up on his music . . . the first song I remember my dad playing for me was "Thunder Road," on the *Greatest Hits* CD. As I grew up, I learned to appreciate the music more and more. My dad was diagnosed with MS before I was born. As I got older, he began to get sicker, and was eventually put in the hospital, unable to walk or use his arms. My sister and I were there with him all the time and he would always ask my mom

to put on his Bruce CDs. *The Rising* album came out when he was in the hospital, and I still remember listening to it with him for the first time. I can't really describe it, but I remember not saying a word the whole time the album ran. . . . Bruce began to be extremely important to me. . . . I began to start my own Bruce collection, and his music helped me a lot when my dad was sick. My father passed away almost three years ago, and *The Rising* was the album that got me through it. Some of my best times with my dad I associate with Bruce, because his music was always in the background. I remember his face when his cousin brought him a t-shirt from *The Rising* Tour . . . I hadn't seen him smile like that in a while. Hearing "Thunder Road" live in Hamilton was absolutely incredible—I couldn't help but cry, I was extremely moved, and felt like my dad was there somehow. The last few years have been rough for me, and I can honestly say that—at times—as strange as it sounds, I felt like Bruce was my best friend, and the only one who understood what I felt, because I heard it all in his songs. So as much as I love the rock 'n' roll aspect to his songs, the words that he has written have meant so much more to me, and really helped shape who I am today.

This notion of Bruce "understanding" who his fans are, what they are going through, is a strand that runs through many fan stories and no doubt accounts for much of the emotional attachment many fans feel.

Passiacfactory says that a Springsteen performance gives "a chance for my old heart to beat young again." Misadventure says the shows are "communal rituals . . . it's not unlike church. It's also a sort of contact—communion. Bruce responds to his audience . . . he feeds off of us and we feed off of him." Another younger fan, Doah, says:

It's not just simply good rock 'n' roll. I find it more like a spiritual experience. I would also swear that there's some sort of chemical reaction that occurs in my body that causes euphoria! I know I've mentioned the "spiritual" word to you before, but I mean it. The only other analogy I can come up with is a drug. My wife has asked me before, "Honey, do you have to see him more than once a week? You're seeing him Monday, why do you have to see him on Tuesday?" I'm like, well, does a heroin addict say, "you know, I already shot up last night so I think I'll pass tonight." I don't think so!

Again, euphoria is also something found in the evangelical experience of being "born again." In this sense, fans are "born anew" at each performance they attend. Other comments state that seeing Springsteen recharges spiritual and emotional batteries. As TheMusicTraveler said: "The need to hear him live kept me alive. It still does. They [the live performances] carry me to a place where all is good and the love for mankind is strong. What could be sweeter?"

The faithful all have a "come-to-Bruce" story that usually involves hearing a particular song for the first time. "I went home and put on side one. . . .

I didn't play anything but side two for a month" (skin2). Some stories are a bit more involved and poignant, such as NC's:

> In Dec. 1980 I moved to Palmer, Alaska. I was miserable because I had to leave my school & friends. I hated it here. It was a small town about 40 miles from Anchorage. The night before John Lennon was shot [12/8/80] I was in my room and found on the top shelve of my closet an old clock radio. I remember the color was a God-awful dull yellow. Wasn't sure if it even worked but I plugged it in. Sure enough it worked. I was able to pick up an album-oriented rock station out of Anchorage. At 10:00 PM every Sunday they would play an album in its entirety. As fate would have it that Sun. night they played *The River.* BOTH ALBUMS! Anyway, that night I was in my room with the lights off and the curtains open watching the aurora borealis and I listened to every song . . . every word. Sometimes I think back and wonder what if I had not found that old clock radio in my closet.

Redheadfromtoronto remembers hearing the title song from the album mentioned above, "The River," on her grandmother's white kitchen radio and being "haunted by the ending." ("Now those memories come back to haunt me / they haunt me like a curse / Is a dream a lie if it don't come true / or is it something worse")

Leahinjersey says she first identified with the *Tunnel of Love* album, written during a time of emotional turmoil for Springsteen, "because I was going through a divorce from my first husband, some major depression." Whoresandgamblers' story started with the *Live 75–85* set of albums: "the songs the stories of teenage angst. Dedicating a song to the young people 'Because the next time they are going to be looking to you, and you will need a lot of information to know what you are going to do.' . . . Everything was like Bruce speaking directly to me." Some years later, this man and his wife were separating, and he

> grabbed a random tape and stuck it in. "Darkness [on the Edge of Town]" was playing and while I had heard the song many times before, something struck a chord in the lyrics to that song. Suddenly my Bruceness was rededicated. LINYC [*Live in New York City,* a DVD] picked up where *Live 75–85* left off. It was different, things had changed people had grown up, but Bruce was there singing directly to me and knowing exactly what I needed to hear. It took me to 2002 to get to a live show but I have since been to 8. Bruce music has been the soundtrack of my life.

This idea of a personalized performance, "playing what I needed to hear" also runs through many fan stories, an echo of sorts of a divine guidance. This person does not say "playing what I wanted to hear" but rather "what I needed to hear," as if there was a close, personal connection between Bruce and himself, which would account for Springsteen knowing what state of mind and life situation this man was in. As one unidentified follower put it: "It's like he's walking around inside my heart looking for song ideas."

BigOldDinosaur says that after seeing a show, "I was completely hooked. I'd never seen someone perform with such energy, just laying it all out there like that. Four days later I went to Utica, and the odyssey had begun and is still continuing 160+ shows later."

And chestercat, a late-comer to the fold, has this to say about her first concert at the age of 40 in 2002: "A couple of bars into the first song, I got hit by something. I started to sob and cried pretty much through the whole thing. Roostershmoo and I went back the next night." Other fans speak of being "baptized in the fires of the majesty, the ministry of rock 'n' roll." The passion and fervor that fills these fan-recollections is obvious, potent, and reminiscent of the religious fever of a revival meeting. The sentiments of unigus sum up the feelings of most in the Springsteen community, but more pointedly those participants on the various Internet sites:

> Bruce has always been the soundtrack of my life . . . he has always vocalized my thoughts, fears, hopes, and dreams. His songs always remind me of people and places, connecting me in ways I never would have fathomed, bringing me to a better/higher realization and recognition. . . . I am so thankful that I'm in the presence of friends that I will never have to explain that to cause you to GET IT.

This is a common sentiment repeated over and over by fans, regardless of their geographical location, gender, sexual orientation, or social class—that Bruce has provided them with the music that chronicles and benchmarks their lives, that Bruce "understands" them. The vast majority of all fans I've spoken with over the years has expressed these feelings. Given that Springsteen has long been called the quintessential "American" artist, I found it curious that fans in other countries would also feel this way. Invariably, however, when I questioned fans in Germany and France about this, and what they found to identify with in Bruce's music, their answers dismissed his "American-ness" and focused on his humanity and the greater human themes of love and sorrow, rejection and redemption, fulfillment and disappointment. As GoCartMozart said:

> There may be other musicians who make "feel good" music. But nobody else who comes right out and stares the pain of living right in the face, then shows you how to move past that and to realize that "It ain't no sin to be glad you're alive," that faith "will be rewarded" and will allow you to stand your ground when the twister comes "to blow everything down." Everybody has heard the clichés. "That which doesn't kill me only makes me stronger." "God never gives you more than you can handle." "It takes the pain and sadness in the world for you to truly appreci-

ate the joy, beauty, and happiness." . . . But Bruce makes you actually FEEL the truth behind them. Pain and joy—what it means to be truly alive. It's so easy to start dying "little by little" in order to anaesthetize the pain. And there are so many ways to do it, drugs being only the most obvious. Bruce reminds us that down that path is death—point blank, right between the eyes. That the best way to deal with pain is to feel it, accept it, learn from it, and move on by experiencing all the joy that life has to offer.

Chapter 9

Sacred Music, Contagious Ecstasy

When I was little and the bells would ring during mass and everyone would put their right arms to their hearts and gently tap, I thought it was funny. Then Sister Mary Jane Bosco told me God walked into the church when the bells tinkled and I stopped laughing. (westcoastgirl)

*U*sing music as a means or pipeline to a spiritual/religious experience is not an uncommon practice. Most spiritual traditions and rituals have a music component of some sort—whether chanting text or sutras, or singing hymns of praise. In the Vaisnava tradition of Hinduism, the practice of *kirtan*, a chanting call and response of mantras over percussion and other instruments, illustrates worship of and devotion to Krishna; kirtan has been practiced for over 500 years (http://kirtan.org) and is one of the pillars of Sikhism, with spiritual adherents expected to listen or sing as part of their worship ritual. In the Jewish faith, various types of music are used for different purposes in different parts of the worship service. New Religious Movements also follow this pattern. The Celebration Center for Spiritual Living (celebrationcenter.org), in West Falls, Virginia, has the following music ministry vision, mission, and purpose statements:

Vision
All who enter the doors of Celebration Center are uplifted by experiencing the joyful expression of music that touches their hearts and feeds their souls.

Mission
To provide a wide variety of high quality music coordinated well in advance, so that there is continuity and flow throughout presentations. This music inspires and uplifts every person who comes to celebrate the Divine with us.

Purpose
To provide excellent music that energizes, uplifts, inspires, soothes, and arouses joy, love, calm, laughter and serenity, and to support individuals in growing into and sharing their gifts and talents . . . (Celebration Center [online])

Springsteen concerts provide the audience with just these things—inspiration, joy, love, a feeling of support—and the fans are indeed "uplifted by the joyful expression of music that touches their hearts and feeds their souls . . . celebrating the Divine." As Jon Stewart said, "Bruce Springsteen is . . . sheer unbridled, unadulterated joy" (Kennedy Center Honors introduction of Bruce Springsteen [online]).

In her book *Dancing in the Streets: A History of Collective Joy*, Barbara Ehrenreich postulates that humans have a need to experience what she calls "collective joy." Throughout humankind's history, one very elemental—and nearly universal, at least outside of the "civilized, western world"—way of finding and expressing this joy was through ecstatic rituals of music and dance (Ehrenreich 2006:1). As anthropologists began to study native populations and their practices and observed these rituals, they often dismissed them as lurid and pointless, "without any sort of meaning" (Melville in Ehrenreich 2006:2). These ubiquitous rites were similar, with observed "extraordinary uniformity" (Ehrenreich 2006:1). Yet the ancient Greeks, the most "rational and Western" of ancient peoples danced their religion, with the devotees of Dionysius dancing themselves into trance states: "The fact that the Greeks felt the need for such a deity tells us something about the importance of ecstatic experience in their world . . . they needed a god to give the experience of ecstasy a human form and face" (Ehrenreich 2006:33). And *The Bacchae* of Euripides says: "Blessed are the dancers and those who are purified, who dance on the hill in the holy dance of god" (Van Ness, 1996:216).

When the slave trade brought slaves from Africa to the United States, the African natives came with their specific cultural and religious beliefs and rituals. Music, drumming, and dance were vital components of their traditions. While many slave owners saw these behaviors as little more than drunken orgies, some observers saw them as "indescribable expressions of ecstasy," felt themselves drawn to the rituals, and "infected unconsciously" (Olmstead in Ehrenreich 2006:3) by "the voice of that world between which is hid from man's sight and hearing" (Ehrenreich 2006:4). In 1920, a visitor in South

Carolina, after having watched an African American *ring-shout*, a religious dance, said:

> A rhythm was born, almost without reference to the words of the preacher. It seemed to take place almost visibly, and grow. I was gripped with the feeling of mass-intelligence, a self-conscious entity, gradually informing the crowd and taking possession of every mind there, including my own. . . . I felt as if some conscious plan or purpose were carrying us along, call it mob-mind, communal composition, or what you will. (Ehrenreich 2006:4)

In some instances, these practices resulted in the participants entering trance states, speaking in strange voices, twisting their bodies into impossible positions, seeing visions, and so forth. Erika Bourguignon wrote in 1963 that "92 percent of small scale societies surveyed encouraged some kind of religious trances . . . through ecstatic group ritual"; but instances of this same sort of ecstatic worship have appeared in the Christian religion (in Ehrenreich 2006:7). Carnival celebrations, religious celebrations that allow for behavior not ordinarily accepted—the population falling "victim" to the contagion of carnival and behaving outside their norm—stand out as another example of non-Western practices.

Social scientists eventually began to make class distinction parallels between Western society's underclass and other cultures. According to Ehrenreich (2006), this contagious ecstasy, group ecstasy, happened to the uneducated, the poor, the "other," and implied a weakness of mind. But as equality became the word of the day and terms such as "primitive" and "savage" fell out of use, the behaviors leading to this state of ecstasy became less foreign. Anthropologists entertained the idea that anyone might experience or even need these rites, acknowledging the possibility that these rites and rituals could possibly be ways of maintaining community. Victor Turner saw collective ecstasy as universally experienced and an expression of communitas, the love and support in a community of equals. The function of the ecstatic ritual, Turner believed, was to work as an occasional release, preventing the community from becoming too rigid (in Ehrenreich 2006:11). Springsteen fans experience this participation in ritual and community-building in their audience activities. As one fan says:

> 20,000 of us raising our hands in the air at all the right moments, we know when to "whoa oh, whoa oh, whoa oh, yea, yea, yea" during "Out in the Street." We raise our hands and sing "Badlands whoa whoa whoa" in unison. We dance at his concerts like nobody's watching. What a feeling! It's liberating and invigorating and makes you feel alive! (Toots)

"That is my mission in this book: to speak seriously of the largely ignored and perhaps incommunicable thrill of the group deliberately united in joy and exaltation" (Ehrenreich 2006:16).

United in joy and exaltation—sounds like a Springsteen show. As in any culture, the rites and ritual practices of a Springsteen fan are specific to the Springsteen community, situationally particular and looking strange to outsiders. Émile Durkheim wrote of "collective effervescence: the ritually induced passion or ecstasy that cements social bonds and . . . forms the ultimate basis of religion" (in Ehrenreich 2006:2). Ehrenreich proposes in her book that we in the Western world have lost our capacity for experiencing collective joy, that we have effectively suppressed this human emotion, much to our own detriment. For Jean Duvignaud, a French sociologist, "Market economies and increasing industrialization are crystallizing the social conditions for eliminating such manifestations (festivities)" (Duvignaud in Ehrenreich 2006:249). The present-day enemy of festivals and ecstatic rituals is social hierarchy; the group in power feels threatened by the rituals that empower the subordinate group, and rituals are viewed as a threat to the "civil order" (Ehrenreich, 2006:251). Elites, she says, "cringe from the spectacle of disorderly public joy" (Ehrenreich 2006:252). It would seem that while festivity is inclusive, hierarchy fosters exclusion, giving way to a divide-and-conquer mentality.

Another way of understanding this "joy" is to consider the idea of bliss. Peter Van Ness (1996) believes that current religious practice has become disconnected from bliss, the "experiences of supreme well-being . . . the joy of being extraordinarily alive" (215). He goes on to say that intense religious joy now appears "mad" and that rationality reigns supreme (215). Bliss is the "embodied fruit of God's blessing" (218), but the word itself has been stripped of any religious meaning and instead relegated to a secular and less "holy" inference. Van Ness sees this separation of intense joy and religious experience as cause for alarm, and that what is left is moralism: "It [religion] becomes more a matter of telling others what they should do by invoking God's authority than of showing others what they can be by realizing God's power" (219). For Springsteen fans, the experience of a live concert translates into this joy, this bliss. For many, the energy transfer between fan and Springsteen translates into action, helping fuel fans' good works. In this sense, he (Springsteen) has shown the audience what they can "be."

Yogic traditions of India incorporated the search for bliss in their meditation practices, seeking *samadhi*, a state of higher consciousness; the highest stage of samadhi is *ananda*, a Sanskrit word that translates as bliss, while the Bhagavad Gita recognizes bliss as the "hallmark of a spiritually disciplined life" (Van Ness 1996:219). One fan, a yoga practitioner who lives in an ashram in Germany, relayed the following experience to me when I inquired how he related to Bruce:

> I think it feels quite esoteric in some way, so I am a little hesitant in talking about it. When I was watching the 1975 London Hammersmith show

early one summer evening, I put on "Backstreets" to show the intensity of Bruce to my wife (who until then—it was last summer—was not too familiar with him). We lay on the bed with the kids, looking at the screen, when the band played the intro, the piano part by Roy . . . the drums starting to roll . . . I started to breath heavily, more rapidly . . . like "Holotopic Breathing.". . . I hyperventilated for quite some seconds till the intro finished building up . . . then *burst* into tears, when the song really opened with the first guitar power chords by Bruce. Yogis would describe this somehow as "energy" experience. . . . I see it happen many times in our Satsang-hall when they chant Mantras just . . . this was not Sanskrit sounds but rock 'n' roll. . . . I have these experiences sometimes (rarely) in meditation . . . I am thankful—but I do not know what was set free in that moment. I am just happy that this musician from the states played some chords with a feeling 35 years back, that brighten my life and free my emotions today. (RS)

The use of music in contemporary organized religion has become critical. The Roman Catholic Church in the United States, desperate to hold on to a dwindling congregation, reached out to folk and rock music and local musicians in order to create a liturgy that responds to the changing culture of their congregations. Moreover, the Catholic Church in Maya Chiapas, Mexico, incorporates not just the sacred music of the Maya but also the rhythmic and repetitive movements of in-place dance (Simonelli 2007). The priest comes down off the altar to join the congregation as they sway and step to traditional song. This is similar to what happens when Springsteen joins the audience in the Pit during certain significant songs. For much of the last half of his *Working on a Dream* Tour in 2009, Springsteen walked into the audience and climbed on a riser in the midst of the audience. Still singing, he would fall back into the audience, confident that they would catch him—which they did. The crowd would them pass him over their heads and back to the stage. The first time I witnessed this maneuver was at Giants Stadium, a football stadium of massive proportions, and Springsteen crowd-surfed a quarter of a football field. His trust in his fans seemed unquestionable—how else, why else would he have done this?

An emotional bonding can be experienced in huge spectacles (or a Springsteen concert) by many thousands of people at once (Ehrenreich 2006). The joy fans find at a Springsteen performance is the glue that holds our fan community together, cements the social bonds between members, and creates a feeling of common fellowship, further mimicking a religious community. Just so, songs are interpreted by the Springsteen fan base as things of reverence, "our sacred music." On his 2009 tour, Bruce led the singers in the band into the audience during the repeated closing song, "Higher and Higher," creating a revival-like atmosphere. Springsteen's performance of this song, along with his triumphant trek through the audience, resembles nothing so much as a spiritual celebration of mutual love. Bruce and band members reached out, shaking hands and connecting with the audience in a way not usually seen in a concert, enlarging the experience of those closest to the action. Hands reaching out toward Bruce are reminiscent of supplicants stretching to touch a Yogi's garment, perhaps hoping for a contagious sort of grace or peace, a variation of the laying on of hands in spiritual healing rituals. In Medieval Christianity, worshipers would often report feeling "infused" with well-being after touching a holy relic of a saint or a cross fragment purportedly from Christ's cross (Van Ness 1996). Congregants in the Springsteen audience may well experience something that carries echoes of this. Brushing fingertips, shaking hands, grasping a calf, or participating in a crowd-surfing relay of Springsteen back to the stage allows the audience access to "our holy relic." And the call-and-response practiced between Springsteen and the audience during many songs also bears more than a passing resemblance to both an old-time sing-along and an African Methodist Episcopal Church worship service.

The Last Dance

> Of course we all grow up and we know "it's only rock and roll" . . . but it's not. After a lifetime of watching a man perform his miracle for you, night after night, it feels an awful lot like love. (Bruce Springsteen, Eulogy for D. Federici)

The year 2009 saw Bruce Springsteen and the E Street Band on tour, purportedly promoting their newest album, *Working on a Dream,* yet on most nights only two or three songs from this album were performed. As the tour developed, Bruce incorporated a "Stump the Band" segment into the show, and fans began holding signs requesting obscure and rarely performed Springsteen songs, as well as other peoples' songs, in an attempt to find tunes that the group could not perform on cue. At a point in the evening, the band would begin to play a song, often "Raise Your Hand" but occasionally a snippet of something else—"Heatwave" or "Green Onions." Bruce would address the audience, saying "Lemme see what you got"—and begin collecting signs. As the tour went along, the signs became more imaginative and plentiful, and the song requests more diverse. According to word of mouth from fans, these signs now reside in a box somewhere, as Bruce is said to have kept them all.

While Springsteen is well-known for deviating from his projected set-list and calling *audibles*—songs not scheduled for performance that night—this most recent variation in the show created a free-wheeling, spontaneous musical atmosphere. The band covered songs ranging from artists like Elvis Presley ("Jailhouse Rock," 10/2/09, Giants Stadium) to the Clash ("London Calling," 4/29/09, Philadelphia Spectrum), from The Who ("My Generation," 5/08/09, at Penn State Bryce Jordan Center) to Chuck Berry ("Roll Over Beethoven," 10/25/09, St. Louis, Missouri) to Van Morrison ("Brown-eyed Girl," 11/3/09, Charlotte), and sealed the mighty E Street Band's well-earned reputation as the "best little bar band ever." Both Springsteen and his audiences seemed to enjoy this musical exercise immensely, and it is likely that the signs had some influence on Springsteen's decision to play entire albums during the last two months on tour. And Springsteen himself expressed the idea that he and the band wanted to do something special for their fans.

From September 2009 until the tour ended in Buffalo on November 22, Springsteen and E Street performed six albums in their entirety. *Born To Run* was played first in Chicago to positive reviews, and in the next weeks, Springsteen management announced that the albums *Darkness on the Edge of Town* and *Born in the U.S.A.* would be added to the playlists in different cities. This created some consternation among fans who traveled to multiple shows. Tickets for the tour routinely went on sale months before a concert date, and consequently some fans saw multiple performances of the same album. For many in the Springsteen community, this seemed a harbinger of things to come. Some fans began to believe that Bruce was playing these albums as a thank you and saw this as a potential sign that this might be the last grand-tour—a farewell tour—of the E Street Band, given the age and health concerns of various members.

A weekend set of concerts at New York City's Madison Square Garden (MSG) saw Springsteen and band re-creating their second album release, the jazzy *The Wild, The Innocent, and The E Street Shuffle,* on night one, and the epic beloved double-disk album *The River* on night two (November 7 & 8, 2009). When it was announced in early November 2009, only four days before the scheduled weekend engagement at New York's MSG, Springsteen nation exploded in a frenzy of anticipation. These albums contained rare songs played little or never in concert, and so the devoted fans who hadn't planned to attend MSG when tickets for the shows went on sale began frantically maneuvering for transportation and tickets, while those of us lucky enough to already have tickets counted our blessings.

I had tickets to attend both shows, but life had gotten in the way, and I needed to sell my Sunday-night ticket for the performance of *The River.* This album strikes a chord with many members of E Street nation, perhaps because of its universal themes. A description of "Wreck on the Highway" by Springsteen himself (2003:101) offers a glimpse at its appeal: "You have a limited number of opportunities to love someone, to do your work, to be a

part of something, to parent your children, to do something good." I posted
on several Web sites that I had an extra to sell and, within hours, had made
arrangements to meet Rollo in New York City that Saturday at a gathering
organized by members of the Web site greasylake.org. A young man in his
mid-thirties, Rollo was flying to New York from Germany, and he intended
to be at both shows in spite of yet having no tickets. As Bruce-luck would
have it, I was able to connect him with a friend of mine who had extra tickets
for Saturday night, so Rollo was set for the weekend. He explained to me that
these two albums had special significance for him, and that even though he
made less than 300 Euros a month working as a yoga teacher at an ashram in
Germany, he felt that he had to be at these shows: "I feel this whole three-
day-trip to NYC is giving a great blast to my personal evolvement as a human
being . . . learning to 'trust' that I will get into the door at MSG, 'letting go' of
fear not to be able to be in the pit. . . . It is a miracle that I can afford to fly in
anyway" (personal correspondence). Rollo spoke to me about his differently
abled stepson who watches "Bruce DVDs with me—and learning to use his
arms to play imaginary guitar is his biggest happiness (next to the love of his
mother, probably)."

The gathering organized by the greasylakers turned out to be a rather large
one. Unlike most U.S. meet-ups, this one was dominated by the European Lak-
ers who'd come over for the MSG shows from Germany, Australia, England,
Wales, Ireland, Scotland, Italy, Sweden, France, and North Wales (apparently
as important a designation to someone from Wales as being an "Upstater" is
to a New Yorker). One Laker assumed the responsibility of making name tags,
complete with flag of origin, so that we would more readily identify each other.
About 40-odd members of greasylake.org attended, with ages ranging from 18
to somewhere north of 60. (The experience can be read in its entirety at
www.greasylake.org/the-circuit/index.php?showtopic=93087&st=0.)

The expectations of the fans for these two concerts were that they would
be exceptional and transcendent; comments after the shows indicate both the
fulfillment of these expectations as well as the emotional and spiritual experiences. Says LOFG:

> I was at night 1 and honestly, started to cry the second he came out,
> although I was singing and dancing all night long. I really lost it during
> Sandy, and was mesmerized for the Incident-Rosie-NYCS trilogy, proba-
> bly the highlight of my concert going career. I could not stop talking
> about how special it was, how it wasn't the usual energy, let's have fun on
> a Saturday night show, but it was something for the ages. Tante texted me
> she was honored to be in the building, and that sums it up.

JT, a male fan said, "To sum that show in one word? Magic." ENJ said:
"This was a man who is known for respecting his audience . . . respecting

them even more that night . . . and sort of giving his legacy an extra tight hug." Canadianfan told me:

> This afternoon, I heard this program on the radio—where the author of a book spoke about the loss we have as a society since we no longer have communal moments of joy. I suspect that the MSG shows tapped into that need in a particular way, in that many of the folks in attendance were aware of the subtext—they had an ongoing long term connection with each other and Bruce and the band—and were also poignantly aware of the passage of time, as evidenced by the loss on stage of one of the original players—and the knowledge that these shows might be the last shows like this.

RHFT said:

> I personally connect with *The River* a lot so that evening, although there were lots of people around me, I found that I was going deep inside myself, my past, my successes and failures. Bruce was talking to me. I cried a lot of tears that night.

For fan NJ1:

> I originally bought my tickets to NYC because of the chance to spend a weekend seeing Bruce with some friends I'd been seeing shows with since '92. With the announcement of the *WIESS* and *River* albums, I felt like I'd won the lottery. The group of friends expanded and that made it even better. *WIESS* has always been my album. . . . And I can't imagine anything surpassing it being played. Not just the songs, but the arrangements and the performance were stellar. . . . I could've gone home after NYC Serenade and been completely sated. . . . MSG1 was the epic and MSG2 was the celebration. While I've seen some great shows by any other standard, those two shows brought back the magic of Bruce and the ESB to a high that I'd forgotten existed.

Each night included songs rarely or never played in concert over the past several decades, and was greeted with reverence and awe by the audience. The experiences varied for the different fans, on the different nights. Said sujormik:

> I found these shows amazing. Saturday and Sunday very different for me. Saturday felt much more physical. . . . *River* was different, very emotional . . . the depth of the emotions. It was like Bruce could sense it.

My response:

> I felt that "One" . . . I felt like I touched the ineffable. . . . I feel like my "attachment" to the songs comes from the feelings they *evoke,* rather than *recall* . . . which makes it different. Maybe that's why it feels, well, *spiritual* to me. . . . I mean, sure, some songs are just pure release & fun, some are romantic, but some of the songs are galaxies unto themselves, little universes where life plays out—and they feel, I dunno, *grander,* more

holy, if you will . . . songs that sound like they came from an angel's soul, full of the bittersweet after-taste of life and yearning for what will now never be . . . all attempts to intellectualize a visceral experience are doomed to failure . . . words aren't enough . . . maybe it is that for that fleeting moment frozen in time we believe we've bridged the existential predicament, the gulf between self and other . . . that's kinda how it felt to me—like the place was whole, one.

FanX said:

Suddenly I'm freakin 17 . . . but what the hell it's Saturday night and I'm in NYC at a Bruce Springsteen show and if I've learned nothing else from Bruce all these years it's that you got to live right here, right now because tomorrow never knows. And what the hell, Bruce is acting like he's 17 the way he is laughing and carrying on up there. But here's the thing, you know how you always wish you could go back and do it all over with the knowledge you have now? That's it! There I was on the floor feeling all of 17 but with the knowledge of considerably more years and the wisdom to just go with the feeling and not worry about anything else. It was an amazing good and powerful feeling. . . . Joy, Love, Hope, Beauty in the music, Friendship, it was all there. Sometime in the far future, I will be in a bad place and I will remember that moment as one of the best in my life. That is what Bruce gave to me.

In a discussion of these shows on the fan-board greasylake.org, cybercat6 posted "Night one was sacred . . . a Communion as I'd never felt so deeply before. I shared a religious experience with some thousands of people." Another poster, MSG9/79, said:

Somehow, some way, they put us in the Time Machine, and they and we were as we felt back then. It was a lot of care and feeding (like Saturday night) that went into this "gift" (yes we paid, but we got much more than a typical great Bruce show). . . . I saw big, tough, jaded guys put down their beers and wipe away tears during the latter. I cannot do it justice. I am still buzzing. And I still cannot believe that at 47, I felt like that 18 yr old. It was magic, it was fun, it was shared joy, and it was one of a kind.

Later, this fan also said:

Everyone knew their part, how to act, and just exuded a connection I cannot explain. I'm a flow and vibe person. It was one of the strongest ones I've ever felt. . . . I have never been part of a group like that. . . . How does he do it? And how did we do it across the board from the seats and the floor area?

These observations would indicate that the hard-core fans present experienced what they self-describe as a communal experience.

Joy is contagious. Scooter101 said: "It was much more than music and to share that with the ones you love (like my wife) and friends from GL you've met on the way and that you know this music means as much to them as it does to you . . . it simply doesn't get any better."

This, in a nutshell, encapsulates much of what the dedicated members of the Church of Bruce feel during a performance—that we have melded with the ineffable.

The music is sacred to fans, and the requisite hand motions act as the accompanying ritual. Says westcoastgirl on greasylake.org:

> As an adult I have come to appreciate the beauty and comfort of ritual. My ritual just happens to be knowing my "parts" at a Bruce show. On Saturday and Sunday nights everyone knew their parts better than I have ever seen, heard or felt.

The gestures used in audience participation and knowing what to do strengthens the idea of being part of a congregation or community of similar minded people. MSG 9/79 noted that "Everyone knew their part, how to act, and just exuded a connection I cannot explain." Judgejudge explains personal feelings about these two nights in a more fanciful, but as sincerely heartfelt, way:

> Yes indeed, nite 1 They went Deep into the TOMBS and recovered the Treasure from the second oldest temple in Ancient New Jersey before the days of Madam Marie and nite 2 they got out the Sonar devices and went miles and miles off the Jersey Shore to a sunken ship that was carrying treasures from the Dutch Irish God of Springsteen and books of knowledge from Italy where God of Love and Giving inspired the good people in the town of Zirelli and these gifts were brought to The Madison Square Garden for the faithful to be Enlightened [Note: Zirelli is Bruce's mother's maiden name].

There is a familiarity and comfort that comes from participation, from pumping fists at the right moment or singing a chorus when you know it is expected. Just as a Catholic parishioner might find comfort in the rite of communion, or in kneeling at specific parts of the service, so do we find comfort in the raised hands around us as we heartily sing a refrain—"May your strength give us strength," or add a hardy "Whoo whoo!" at Bruce's signal. The inclusiveness of performing these gestures is not to be dismissed, as the doing becomes a signifier of who is—and who is not—a member of the congregation, and therefore identifiable as a friend and comrade. Fan M expressed it this way, when asked about singing along: "It was like our shared secret or something. You lock eyes with a stranger at a show singing along to 'Incident,' and there is this connection, like you both know something that the rest of your seating section is missing out on." Most fans posting on the Springsteen fan sites around the Internet mentioned this connection felt, one fan to another. JimT on greasylake.org noted that Bruce seemed to make an individual connection with every fan in the venue: "No matter how large the crowd you feel those moments where the connection is personal, one-to-one." This bridging between the performer and the fan is a fleeting momentary negation of the existential predicament, that inability to bridge the gap between self and other. This feeling is difficult to capture in words, but misadventure from greasylake.org likens the feeling to reciprocity, a sharing of experience:

> When we respond he responds more and it just feeds on itself. It's almost as though we've all become some larger corporate being . . . audience and Bruce. And I think in some ways, that reciprocity is what people describe when they have spiritual experiences. Those are the moments when not only do we pray to God (if we're religious/spiritual) but we actually feel as though he's listening, as though he's stepped into the vicinity. I know it kind of sounds like I'm equating Bruce with God here and I don't mean to do that; I think he's the instrument as are we. I mean that together, as audience and performer, we become a larger being . . . larger than the sum of our parts. It seems as though he's really hungry to connect with as many of us on a one-to-one basis as he possibly can.

FanQ, from outside the United States, said of the second night at MSG and the performance of *The River:*

> I don't have words to describe it, not even in my own language. It's been an *experience*, that much is certain, maybe *the* experience. It gave joy, happiness, a sense of rejuvenation and the sort of strength that is associated with it. It crossed my mind that this night perhaps could be compared to the completion of the Grail quest, the search for the "holy grail" in Christian mythology? Maybe for a few of us. (November 30, 2009)

ENJ felt the joy, and his comment speaks to the moment of losing oneself in the music:

> I was so joyous during the rockers that in some sad ways it was like I didn't hear them . . . it was on the slower songs that I allowed myself to sit down and just let the majesty of the ESB wash over me that I was amazed by!!!

Magicrat67 felt: "A week later and I am still trying to wrap my head around what I witnessed last Sunday. You hit it on the head when you mention passion."
And JCt said:

> Yes indeed. The one thing I might add is that the connection of Bruce to each individual in the arena during these shows (during the "sacred music"), and others that I have seen (although these are 2 of my top 3 or 4) was exactly that—individual. No matter how large the crowd you feel those moments where the connection is personal, one-to-one. Not during Rosalita, or a stadium-sing-along of "Twist and Shout"—those moments are different, and enjoyable as well but in a different way. But "Fade

Away," "Price You Pay," "Drive All Night," "Stolen Car," "Wreck"—absolutely personal. Each of us no doubt has "context" for many of those songs (heck, we have 30 *years* of context for "The River")—the first time we heard them on the record, the first time we heard them live, some past relationship. Is there a 40+ year old man who can't listen to "Independence Day" and bring in the context of his relationship with his father (or maybe with his son)?

Several weeks later, the last show of the tour was performed in Buffalo, New York. To mark this occasion, Springsteen and the band performed his first album—*Greetings from Asbury Park*. And while not the show-stopper perhaps that *The Wild, the Innocent, and the E Street Shuffle* or *The River* was, the announcement nonetheless left members of the E Street congregation with feelings of fear and trepidation. Many felt that this playing of the first-ever album perhaps marked the performance of the last-ever concert by Bruce Springsteen and the E Street Band. Fans gathering before the show were discussing the last performance on *The Rising* Tour at Shea Stadium, a three-plus hour long love-fest that ended in tears for the band as well as the audience. A particularly poignant performance of "Blood Brothers" was the culprit responsible, and everyone in Buffalo was expecting something equally sentimental and sad. After all, Bruce had just turned 60, Clarence would be turning 68 in a few months and having major surgery, and Danny was already gone; realistically speaking, how much longer would they practically be able to tour? And so the preshow mood was a trifle more subdued, somber, and bitter-sweet than the normal preshow frenzy. While we were not certain what was in store for us, we all felt the weight of mortality weighing down on Bruce, the band, and ourselves.

Because of the possibility that this might be the very last-ever show configured as we all knew and loved it, fans flocked to Buffalo from all over the globe for this show. One fan traveled from Nova Scotia, while others came from Australia and any number of European countries. One fan from Colorado paid $700 for a concert ticket because he did not want to miss what might be the last performance (Meyer 2009). Max Weinberg's (the E Street drummer) mother drove in from New Jersey to see her son, along with celebrities such as former NBA coach Pat Riley, actress Debra Messing, and NBC's Brian Williams (Meyers 2009). Scalpers on the street were asking—and receiving—upwards of $400 a ticket.

Many of the fans had signs saying "Thank You," or some variation of the same, and held them up at various times during the performance. On the balcony railing in front of my section, two young women hung a sign that said "It's only rock 'n' roll but it feels like love," a quote from Bruce's eulogy at Danny Federici's funeral. While the overall feel was that of less excitement than normal, it was neither sad nor gloomy, just a very different sort of atmosphere for a Springsteen show. As one fan wrote on brucespringsteen.net:

> Most diehard fans in Buffalo tonight hoped for two things. First, for a special, emotional show because this could be the last performance of Bruce Springsteen & the E Street Band. And second, we didn't want it to be the last performance of Bruce Springsteen & the E Street Band. It feels like we got both wishes. (Phillips)

As this comment would indicate, what the fans got was an all-out, hard rockin' show, during which Bruce himself intimated that he was not done with touring. The first request performed that evening was "Hang Up My Rock'n Roll Shoes" (written by Chuck Willis), and during the last song of the evening—and the tour—"Rockin' All Over the World" (written by John Fogerty), Bruce said: "So we're gonna say goodbye, but just for a little while . . . a *very* little while because . . . because . . . I like it, I like it, I like it, I li-li-like it!" The performance was in no way sentimental, maudlin, or melancholy, but rather a farewell-for-a-while exultation and exclamation of love, from fans to the performers, and likewise, and perhaps more importantly, from Bruce to his legion of followers. There were no tears, but smiles all around. Somehow, Springsteen had made this evening an occasion of joy and not sorrow. The performance of "Higher and Higher" (originally performed by Jackie Wilson in 1967) made the love in the room feel nearly tangible, and no true fan present doubted for a moment that what they were experiencing was real. While it may eventually turn out to be the case that the E Street Band as we know it will cease to tour, what those present in Buffalo saw was a tribute to and celebration of a nearly 40-year love affair between musicians and fans.

Conclusion
"Tomorrow There'll Be Sunshine And All This Darkness Past"

Now I'm out here on this road,
Alone on this road tonight.
I close my eyes and feel so many friends around me
in the early evening light.
And the miles we have come,
and the battles won and lost
Are just so many roads traveled,
and just so many rivers crossed.
And I ask God for the strength
and faith in one another.
'Cause it's a good night for a ride
'cross this river to the other side.
My blood brothers.
("Blood Brothers," in a concert of *The Rising* Tour)

This ethnography has documented the ways in which fans have created a community and a spiritual home for themselves, open and welcoming to all those likewise inspired by the words, music, and actions of Bruce Springsteen. Springsteen has himself laid the groundwork for this and consequently can claim some credit for the positive ways in which his fans are working toward

maintaining this community and doing good works in the world. To para-
phrase Springsteen, the world we carry in our hearts is waiting; we just need
to help manifest its potential greatness. By their own accounts, these congregants have been supplied with spiritual/emotional sustenance, gaining solace,
redemption, and companionship in some fashion equal to the comfort and
companionship provided by church congregations or ministerial counseling.
Bruce says this is his job:

> That's my business, that's what it's all about—trying to connect to you. It
> comes down to trying to make people happy, feel less lonely, but also
> about being a conduit for a dialogue about the events of the day, the
> issues that impact people's lives, personal and social and political and
> religious. That's how I always saw the job of our band. That was my
> service . . . I can't do it by myself. I need my audience. You're in that
> room together, that dark room together. (in Levy 2007:52)

For this man Bruce Springsteen rock 'n' roll is serious business, sacred
business. "What are the things that bring you ecstasy and bliss, what are the
things that bring on the darkness . . . what can we do together to combat
those things?" (in Levy 2007:52). His music and performances serve as a
bridge for the faithful to that larger sense of the divine, the light that counters
the darkness, the vehicle for some of that ecstasy and bliss we all need in our
lives. Like a shaman, Bruce serves as an intermediary between our present
selves and what we might become. He helps us transcend the individual to
become part of a collective, a congregation, helping us overcome our stress
and fear—if only for the hours that we share in concert. We get to step out of
our mundane and hectic lives into the sacred space of the concert hall, experiencing the grace and union of understanding, forgiveness, redemption, and
new hope. "Here everybody has a neighbor / Everybody has a friend /
Everybody has a reason to begin again" ("Long Walk Home").

If the truer measure of religion is found in what it does for its believers
rather than what it *is*, then fans are closer to being a congregation than a
mere audience (Mazur and McCarthy 2001:5). For those without close religious affiliations, these connections with Springsteen and other fans represent a way out of isolation and alienation and a way into relationship, a
refuge and comfort from everyday life every bit as legitimate and meaningful
as any religious institution. What Bruce has in common with all of the great
religious leaders throughout time is his way of speaking. Ultimately, when
talking about spiritual leaders, we are talking about storytellers. Buddha,
Jesus, Krishna—their stories captured the people, drew them in and left them
open to the higher truths of existence and faith. And if there is one thing that
Bruce Springsteen is, it is a storyteller of the people. As Sarfraz Manzoor, a
Muslim and devoted Springsteen follower says, Springsteen fans are "defined

not by geography, race, or religion, but by passion" (2007:103). Bossfan950
sums it up:

> In our world of Bruce we get to forget our problems for 2 and a half hours
> or so. We hide on the backstreets and as dogs on Main Street howl, we
> howl and dance and sing and hug and love and live and die in the com-
> pany of our blood brothers and sisters. Thank you Bruce and thank you
> my blood brothers and sisters for being with me on this part of the ride. We
> may all agree to disagree. We have our fights. But in the end we all share
> the music, a bond that we may bend but we cannot and will not break.

Tonight my baby and me we're gonna ride to the sea
And wash these sins off our hands
("Racing In The Street")

Afterword

On April 17, 2008, Danny Federici, organ, accordion, and glockenspiel player with Bruce Springsteen and the E Street Band for over 40 years, lost his battle with melanoma. Since then, fans on the Web site backstreets.com have raised over $12,000 for the Danny Federici Melanoma Fund, more good works focused around Springsteen and his music. Following Danny's death, concerts over the next few months were opened with a video-montage tribute along with Springsteen's personal stories about Danny. This public mourning allowed fans to share the sorrow felt by Bruce and the band, another gesture embracing the fan family. This can be viewed at www.brucespringsteen.net/news/index.html.

It is rumored that Bruce sang "4th of July, Asbury Park (Sandy)" to Danny in the hospital the night before he died.

Bibliography

Albanese, Catherine. *America Religion and Religions*. Belmont, CA: Wadsworth, 1999.

American Heritage Dictionary. New York: Houghton Mifflin, 2001.

Ang, Ien. *Watching* Dallas: *Soap Opera and the Melodramatic Imagination*. New York: Methuen, 1989.

Barna, George, and Mark Hatch. *Boiling Point: Monitoring Cultural Shifts in the 21st Century*. Ventura, CA: Regal, 2003.

Berger, Arthur Asa. *Cultural Criticism: A Primer of Key Concepts*. Thousand Oaks, CA: Sage, 1995.

Berger, Harris M., and Giovanna P. Del Negro. *Identity and Everyday Life: Essays in the Study of Folklore, Music, and Popular Culture*. Middletown, CT: Wesleyan University Press, 2004.

Bernstein, David J. "Aging of the E Street Nation: Springsteen in the 21st Century." Unpublished manuscript. Presented at *Glory Days: A Bruce Springsteen Symposium*, September 25, 2009.

Binelli, Mark. "Bruce Springsteen's American Gospel." *Rolling Stone*, August 22, 2002, 903.

Brown, Susan Love, ed. *Intentional Community: An Anthropological Perspective*. Albany: SUNY Press, 2002.

Bugeja, Michael. *Interpersonal Divide: The Search for Community in a Technological Age*. New York: Oxford University Press, 2005.

Caputo, John D. *On Religion*. New York: Routledge, 2001. Reprinted 2006.

Cavicchi, Daniel. *Tramps Like Us: Music and Meaning Among Springsteen Fans*. New York: Oxford University Press, 1998.

Celano, Claire Marie. "Springsteen Fans Help Build E Street Habitat Home." *Suburban*, August 12, 2004, http://suburban.gmnews.com/news/2004-08-12/Front_page/006.html.

Chang, Suna. "Putting his Money Where His Music Is." *Star-Ledger*, November 24, 1996 www.nj.com/springsteen/stories/charity (accessed August 12, 2008).

Chidester, David. "The Church of Baseball, the Fetish of Coca-Cola, and the Potlatch of Rock 'n' Roll: Theoretical Models for the Study of Popular Religion in

Popular Culture." *Journal of American Academy of Religion* 64, no. 4 (Winter 1996): 743–765.

———. *Authentic Fakes: Religion and American Popular Culture.* Berkeley: University of California Press, 2005.

Cirrincione, Sal. "Greetings from Asbury Park Public Library," ©WORD, August 2003, 12. http://asburyparklibrary.org/?BSS/BSSC_Word.htm (accessed March 12, 2008).

Clark, Lynn Schofield, ed. "Introduction to a Forum on Religion, Popular Music, and Globalization." *Journal for the Scientific Study of Religion* 45, no. 4 (2006): 475–479.

"More Glory Days," President William Jefferson Clinton. July, 2009. *AARP: The Magazine,* http://www.aarpmagazine.org/entertainment/springsteen_more_glory_days.html (accessed October 1, 2009).

Cole, Robert. *Bruce Springsteen's America: The People Listening, a Poet Singing.* New York: Random House, 2003.

Collum, Danny Duncan. "To the River Together: Family and Community at the Bruce Springsteen Show." *Sojourners* 29, no. 4 (2000): 52–56.

Connerton, Paul. *How Societies Remember.* New York: Cambridge University Press, 1989. Reprinted 2002.

Cross, Charles R. and editors of *Backstreets* Magazine. *Backstreets: Springsteen: The Man and His Music.* New York: Harmony Books, 1989.

Croteau, David, and William Hoynes. *Media Society: Industries, Images, and Audiences,* 2nd ed. Thousand Oaks, CA: Pine Forge Press, 2000.

Cullen, Jim. Born in the U.S.A.: *Bruce Springsteen and the American Tradition.* Middletown, CT. Wesleyan University Press, 2005.

Detweiler, Craig, and Barry Taylor. *A Matrix of Meaning: Finding God in Pop Culture.* Grand Rapids, MI: Baker Academic, 2003.

Dettmar, Kevin, and William Richey. *Reading Rock and Roll: Authenticity, Appropriation, Aesthetics.* New York: Columbia University Press, 1999.

Drucker, Jesse. "Springsteen's Life Built on Foundation of Giving—Quietly." *Star Ledger,* August 11, 1999 www.nj.com/springsteen/stories/0811charity (accessed October 10, 2009).

Duffy, John. "Glory Days: Dispatches from an Academic Conference on Bruce Springsteen," September 25, 2009, http://www.Pastemagazine.com (accessed September 27, 2009).

Dunbar-Hall, Peter. "Semiotics as a Method for the Study of Popular Music." *International Review of the Aesthetics and Sociology of Music* 22, no. 2 (December 1991): 127–132.

Earle, Duncan, and Jeanne Simonelli. *Uprising of Hope: Sharing the Zapatista Journey to Alternative Development.* New York: Rowman and Littlefield, 2005.

Ehrenreich, Barbara. *Dancing in the Streets: A History of Collective Joy.* New York: Holt Paperbacks, 2006.

Eliade, Mircea. *The Sacred and the Profane.* New York: Harcourt Brace & World, 1959.

Etzioni, Amitai, ed. *New Communitarian Thinking: Persons, Virtues, Institutions and Communities.* Charlottesville: University Press of Virginia, 1995.

Evans, Christopher H., and William R. Herzog II, eds. *The Faith of 50 Million: Baseball, Religion, and American Culture.* Louisville, KY: Westminster John Knox Press, 2002.

Fanshel, Rosalie Zdzienicka. "Beyond Blood Brothers: Queer Bruce Springsteen." Unpublished paper presented at *Glory Days: A Bruce Springsteen Symposium*, September 25–27, 2009.

Fiske, John. *Reading the Popular.* London: Routledge, 2000.

————. *Understanding Popular Culture.* London: Routledge, 1990.

Forbes, Bruce David, and Jeffrey H. Mahan, eds. *Religion and Popular Culture in America.* Berkeley: University of California Press, 2000.

Garman, Bryan K. A. *Race of Singers: Whitman's Working Class Hero from Guthrie to Springsteen.* Chapel Hill: University of North Carolina Press, 2000.

Geertz, Clifford. *The Interpretation of Cultures.* New York: Basic, 1973.

Goodman, Fred. *The Mansion on the Hill: Dylan, Young, Geffen, Springsteen, and the Head-on Collision of Rock and Commerce.* New York: Random House, 1997.

Graff, Gary, ed. *The Ties That Bind: Bruce Springsteen A to E to Z.* Detroit: Visible Ink Press, 2005.

Grey, Alex. *The Mission of Art.* Boston: Shambhala, 2001.

Greeley, Andrew M. "The Catholic Imagination of Bruce Springsteen." *Black Sacred Music: A Journal of Theomusicology* 6, no.1 (1992): 232–243.

Guilfoile, Kevin. "I Know You're Lonely for Words That I Ain't Spoken." *The Morning News,* August 5, 2002, http://www.themorningnews.org/archives/opinions/i_know_youre_lonely_for_words_that_i_aint_spoken.php.

Guroff, Meg, Jim Jerome, and Lyndon Stambler. "Glory Days: Friends of the Boss Share Their Most Intimate Insights." *AARP: The Magazine,* September/October 2009, 42–43, 72.

Guterman, Jimmy. *Runaway American Dream: Listening to Bruce Springsteen.* Cambridge, MA: De Capo Press, 2005.

Hyman, Mark. "The Boss Grew up Here—But Mum's The Word." *Businessweek,* October 2, 2000, http://www.businessweek.com (accessed December 12, 20080.

Keller, Suzanne. *Community: Pursuing the Dream, Living the Reality.* Princeton: Princeton University Press, 2003.

Kirsch, Lawrence. *For You: Original Stories and Photographs by Bruce Springsteen's Legendary Fans.* Montreal: Lawrence Kirsch Communications, 2007.

————. *The Light in the Darkness.* Montreal: Lawrence Kirsch Communications, 2009.

Kotarba, Joseph A. and John M. Johnson, eds. *Postmodern Existential Sociology.* Walnut Creek, CA: Altamira Press, 2002.

Krause, Michael. "Obituary for a Friend Tears Apart Community of Springsteen Fans." *St. Petersburg Times,* February 28, 2010, http://www.tampabay.com (accessed March 2, 2010).

Leutloff-Grandits, Carolin, An ja Peleikis, and Tatjana Thelen. *Social Security in Religious Networks.* New York: Berghahn Books, 2009.

Levy, Joe. "Bruce Springsteen: The *Rolling Stone* Interview." *Rolling Stone,* November 1, 2007, 51–56.

Lindberg, Peter Jon. "Forever Asbury." *Travel and Leisure,* August 2004, http://www.travelandleisure.com (accessed December 12, 2009).

Lombardi, John. "The Sanctification of Bruce Springsteen and the Rise of Mass Hip." *Esquire:* December 1988.

Lynch, Gordon. *Losing My Religion: Moving on from Evangelical Faith.* London: Darton Longman & Todd, 2004.

———. "The Role of Popular Music in the Construction of Alternative Spiritual Identities and Ideologies." *Journal for the Scientific Study of Religion* 45, no. 4 (2006): 481–488.

Manzoor, Sarfraz. *Greetings from Bury Park: Race, Religion, and Rock and Roll.* London: Bloomsbury, 2007.

Marsh, Dave. *Bruce Springsteen: Two Hearts, the Definitive Biography, 1972–2003.* New York: Routledge, 2004.

Mattingly, Terry. *Pop Goes Religion: Faith in Popular Culture.* Nashville: W Publishing Group, 2005.

Mazur, Eric, Michael McCarthy, and Kate McCarthy. *God in the Details: American Religion and Popular Culture.* New York: Routledge, 2001.

Metcalf, Stephen. "Tunnel of Love: The Right's Unrequited Crush on Bruce Springsteen." *New York,* December 11, 2009, http://nymag.com/news/intelligencer/62673.

Meyer, Brian. "Boss' Faithful are Left to Wonder." *The Buffalo News,* November 24, 2009, http://www.buffalonews.com/home/story/870678.html).

Meyer, Rev. Suzanne. Personal communication, January 21, 2008.

"More Glory Days," Clinton, William Jefferson, President. July, 2009. *AARP: The Magazine,* http://www.aarpmagazine.org/entertainment/springsteen_more_glory_days.html (accessed October 1, 2009.)

New International Webster's Pocket Dictionary of the English Language. Naples, FL: Trident Press International, 1997.

Niebuhr, H. Richard. *Faith on Earth.* New Haven: Yale University Press, 1989.

Pals, Daniel L. *Eight Theories of Religion.* New York: Oxford University Press, 2006.

Pappke, David Ray. "Crime, Lawbreaking, and Counterhegemonic Humanism in the Songs of Bruce Springsteen," Marquette University Law School Legal Studies Research Paper Series. Research Paper No. 06. March 13, 2006.

Partridge, C. *The Re-enchantment of the Wes. Vol 2, Alternative Spiritualities, Sacralization, Popular Culture and Occulture.* London: Continuum, 2005.

Percy, Will. "Rock and Read: Will Percy Interviews Bruce Springsteen," March 29, 2007. http://www.doubletakemagazine.org (accessed April 30, 2007).

Perusse, Bernard. "If You Can't Trust a Bruce Tramp, Then Who Can You Trust?" December 18, 2007, http://www.nationalpost.com (accessed February 23, 2008).

Pew Forum on Religion and Public Life. "First Report on the U.S. Religious Landscape Survey," February 25, 2008, http://pewforum.org/First-Report-on-US-Religious-Landscape-Survey.aspx (accessed May 3, 2010).

Pinn, Anthony B., ed. *Noise and Spirit: The Religious and Spiritual Sensibilities of Rap Music.* New York: New York University Press, 2003.

Price, Mark. "The Boss Gives $50K to Food Bank: Bruce Springsteen Matches Springs Close Foundation's Pledge to Help Area Needy," November 4, 2009, www.heraldonline.com/120/story/1723746.html?story_link=email_msg (accessed November 9, 2009).

Primeaux, Patrick. *The Moral Passion of Bruce Springsteen.* Bethesda, MS: International Scholars, 1996.

Putnam, Robert D. *Bowling Alone: The Collapse and Revival of American Community.* New York: Simon and Schuster, 2000.

Religion and Ethics Newsweekly. "Religion in Europe," July 13, 2001 episode # 446, www.pbs.org/wnet/religionandethics/week446/cover.html (accessed January 28, 2008).

Rheingold, Howard. *Virtual Community: Homesteading on the Electronic Frontier.* Cambridge: MIT press, 1993. 2nd ed. 2002.

Roof, Wade Clark. *Community and Commitment: Religious Plausibility in a Liberal Protestant Church.* New York: Elsevier North Holland, 1978.

Romanowski, William D. *Pop Culture Wars: Religion and the Role of Entertainment in American Life.* Downers Grove, IL: Inter Varsity Press, 1996.

————. *Eyes Wide Open: Looking for God in Popular Culture.* Grand Rapids, MI: Brazos Press, 2001.

Sanders, Joshunda. "Being a Fan of The Boss Is No Passing Thing: A Springsteen Concert Brings out His Life-Long Devotees," August 18, 2003, www.sfgate.com/cgi-in/article.cgi?file=/c/a/2003/08/18/DD63 (accessed March 19, 2008).

Sandford, Christopher. *Springsteen Point Blank.* London: Little, Brown, 1999.

Sawyer, June Skinner, Ed. *Racing In The Street: The Bruce Springsteen Reader.* New York: Penguin Books, 2004.

Shasha, David. "Radical Traditionalism: The Passion of the Artistic in a Time of Crisis." *The American Muslim (TAM),* June 25, 2006, http://theamericanmuslim.org/tam.php/features/articles/readical_traditionalism_the_passion_of_the_artistic_in_a_time_of_crisis/.

Simonelli, Jeanne. "Field of Dreams, Field of Reality: Growing with and in Anthropology." In *Extraordinary Anthropology: Transformations in the Field,* edited by Jean-Guy A. Goulet and Bruce G. Miller, 352–379. Lincoln, NE: University of Nebraska Press 2007.

Smith, Greg. "Whitman, Springsteen, and the American Working Class." *The Midwest Quarterly* 41, no. 3 (Spring 2000): 302–320.

Smith, Larry David. *Bob Dylan, Bruce Springsteen and American Song.* Westport: Praeger, 2002.

Smith, Martha Nell. "Sexual Mobilities in Bruce Springsteen: Performance as Commentary." *South Atlantic Quarterly* 90 (Fall 1991): 833–854.

Somerset, Bruno. "Give Me That Old Time Religion? No Thanks, I've Got Bruce Springsteen." www.associatedcontent.com/article/210033/give_me_that_old_time_religion_no_thanks.html?cat=9 (accessed May 3, 2010).

Springsteen, Bruce. *Songs.* New York: First Harper Entertainment, 2003.

Storey, John. *Cultural Studies and the Study of Popular Culture: Theories and Methods.* Athens: University of Georgia Press, 1996. Reprinted 1998.

Stratton, Christopher. "Springsteen and the Minor Prophets," 2007, www.explorefaith.org/music/springsteen (accessed October 30, 2007).

Strauss, Robert. "When the Feathers Flew, Springsteen Fans Dug Deep." *New York Times* online, November 23, 2003, http://query.nytimes.com/gst/fullpage.html?res=950DE2D8103BF930A15752C 1A96559C8 (accessed March 27, 2007).

Strinati, Dominic. *An Introduction to Theories of Popular Culture.* New York: Routledge, 1995.

Swartley, Ariel. "Red, White, and Bruce." *AARP The Magazine.* Sept/Oct 2009: 38–44.

Swirsky, Chloe, and Marc Perlman." Fandom as a Modern Popular Religion." Unpublished Paper.

"The Lawyer as Poet Advocate: Bruce Springsteen and the American Lawyer," Symposium. *Widener Law Journal* 14, no. 3 (2005).

Tomlinson, John. *Cultural Imperialism: A Critical Introduction.* Baltimore: Johns Hopkins University Press, 1991.

Turner, Victor. *From Ritual to Theatre: The Human Seriousness of Play.* New York: Performing Arts Journal Publishers: 1982.

————. *The Anthropology of Performance.* New York: PAJ, 1986.

Van Ness, Peter. "Endangered Bliss: Reflections on Joy and Religion." *Journal of Religion and Health* 35, no. 3 (1996): 215–223.

Waddell, Ray. "Bruce Springsteen: The Billboard Cover Q & A." www.billboard.com/news/bruce-springsteen-the-billboard-cover-q-1004049585.story (accessed December 12, 2009).

Waldinger, Patrick E. *Going Online to Meet Offline: A Thematic Analysis of Meetup.Com Members' Perceptions of Community.* Winston-Salem, NC: Wake Forest University, 2005.

Walker, Bruce Edward. "Bruce Springsteen: Bringing Charity Back Home," January 28, 2004. Acton Institute for the Study of Religion and Liberty. http://www.acton.org/commentary/commentary_177.php (accessed February 26, 2008).

Watson, C. W., Editor. *Being There.* Sterling, VA: Pluto Press, 1999.

Weider, Judy. "Bruce Springsteen: *The Advocate* Interview." In *Racing In The Street: The Bruce Springsteen Reader,* edited by Judith Skinner Sawyer. New York: Penguin Books, 2004.

Yamin, George Y. Jr. "The Theology of Bruce Springsteen." *Journal of Religious Studies* 16, nos. 1 & 2 (1990): 1–21.

Interviews and Electronic Correspondence

all4eddie	February 29, 2008
Aussiebrucefan	May 28, 2007
badscooter	February 28, 2007
barefootgirl & littlegun	March 10, 2008
BC	December 14, 2009
bigolddinosaur	August 20, 2007
BjorntorunMN	March 16, 2008
blueguitar	April 6, 2003
	October 30, 2007
Brianzai	March 3, 2008
Chestercat	March 1, 2007
	April 16, 2007
CosmicKid	July 25, 2003.
Corvettesue	June 4, 2007
cruisin'tobruce	2001-2009
Deano	March 3, 2008
Doah	February 15, 2008
ENJ	November 7, 2009
FanM	November 10, 2009

FanQ	November 7, 2009
	November 30, 2009
FanX	November 14, 2009
H	February 16, 2008
hanaree	March 7, 2007
happyface	April 8, 2009
hardgirloneasystreet	March 16, 2008
Hobbs	December 13, 2007
JCt	November 14, 2009
Jj	March 12, 2007
JT	November 13, 2009
janiss	December 17, 2007
	October 4, 2009
Joe	March 16, 2008
Judgejudge	November 26, 2009
LOFG	March 23, 2007
Leahinjersey	February 12, 2007
MR	November 22, 2009
Mag	July 12, 2006
Magicrat67	November 14, 2009
misadventure	March 2, 2008
	November, 2009
Mitch	March 10, 2008
Moe_howard2	August 26, 2009
NC	March 2, 2008
Passaicfactory	November, 2009
Pbjcrane	December 13, 2009
RHFT	March 28, 2008
RS	January 28, 2010
Rev.B	February 26, 2008
	March 12, 2008
Roostershmoo	March 1, 2007
S.	May 30, 2007
Scout	March 1, 2007
Skin2	February 2, 2007
SpringsteenMagic	March 15, 2008
Steven	March 16, 2008
sujormik	November 14, 2009
unigus	March 3, 2007
wandasf	March 28, 2008
whoresandgamblers	August 14, 2007

Other E-Contributors

anotherthinline
Bossfan950

bosshawg
cajunboyinthecity
Candaianfan
Carl
cybercat6
D
elvisisalive
ericm104
GoCartMozart
J
Jjmiller
JimT
joanfontaine
killiefrombuffalo
MSG9/79
NJ1
Obxscully
Phillips
Redheadfromtoronto
rosie3030
SH
scooter101
Steven
sujormik
Sweetlight
TheMusicTraveler
Toots
westcoastgirl
westcoast
yark

Web Sites

www.asburyparklibrary.org
www.backstreets.com
www.brucebase.org
http://brucesentme.com
www.brucespringsteen.net
www.celebrationcenter.org
www.greasylake.org
www.greenleaf.uncg.edu
www.hope.ac.uk
www.kennedy-center.org/programs/specialevents/honors/
http://kirtan.org
www.looktothestars.org
www.massmoments.org

http://matt.orel.ws/index.html (Orel family fund)
www.njrockmap.com
www.remind.org
www.rochesterroots.org
www.rollingstone.com
www.spinner.aol.com/rockhall
www.stoneponylondon.net
http://s15.invisionfree.com/ThunderRoad
http://www.trinity-episcopal.org
http://worldpress.com